Transformir
Anchors, Reporters & W
Into Supersta

I0048935

The Craft & Art
of Commanding…

LOYALTY, TRUST
& SUCCESS

by
Bill Cakmis

First Printing, 2020

ISBN 978-0-578-61863-0

CAKMIS
P.O. Box 2762
BRENTWOOD, TN 37024
United States

www.Cakmis.com

Mom, Dad and Zee…

You are the spring that I draw from,
and the spirit that gives it all meaning.

Contents

- Introduction -

You're born with talent.
Technique you gotta earn.

Your success is directly related to your skill as a communicator. That's a fact. In your career. In your social circles. In your personal relationships. And in your life. The stronger you are at interpersonal and group communications, the more apt you will be to win whatever social games life presents to you. If you believe me so far, what will you do when I tell you that this book offers proven techniques that will get you noticed, compel others to listen to you and ultimately propel you to success in your career? Presumably you will read on. Because it will. And you should.

But what if you're an anchor, reporter or weathercaster? Since broadcast news folks are dubious in nature, (it's one of the reasons the great ones are so good at their jobs), there's a chance you may already be thinking that this book probably isn't for you. After all, who is this author, really? And you've already got the communication thing covered, right?

After three decades of coaching performers, actors, anchors, politicians, speakers, talk show hosts, religious leaders and lawyers, I found the most challenging professionals to work with are those in the broadcast news industry. Not because they are dimwitted or incompetent. On the contrary. Local TV and cable news network personalities are some of the smartest, most talented and highly-spirited people I know. The problem usually stems from the fact that they never asked for my help in the first place. Most other clients employ my services themselves, so they are already sold on my abilities and are personally invested in the coaching sessions, determined to get the most out of the experience.

Broadcast news folks, on the other hand, are usually 'scheduled' for their first coaching session by their employers; made to sit in a room with what they believe will be just another 'consultant' (aka Beelzebub) for an hour (precious time that could have been used for more productive pursuits, aka ANYTHING ELSE) and must suffer through a lecture from this dolt who has probably never been on the working end of a microphone, much less in front of a camera. And is most likely 'consulting' because of an ineptitude to do anything else in this business... or in life! Yikes.

Now, in truth, not all first coaching sessions with broadcast news talent begin that way. But a lot do. And the attitude is not all that surprising when you consider how many of these folks began their careers. Out of all the professions I deal with, broadcast news staffers are the only ones who aren't rigorously trained in the art and craft of interpersonal and group communications before taking on a career as, you guessed it... a communicator! Crazy, right? In school they might have taken a public speaking class or were given a few tips on how to behave when the camera was pointed in their direction. But a comprehensive course developing the skills necessary to be a powerful communicator and a success in their industry, just wasn't offered. Like throwing young children who don't know how to swim into a lake, hoping the fear of drowning will be the fastest way of teaching them the backstroke; broadcast news folks, with little technique and even less training, are thrown onto the air waves hoping that the sheer desire to survive will be motivation enough to magically mold them into expert communicators.

Consequently, many of the ones who do survive this rite of passage, do so by mimicking how they think successful anchors or reporters or weathercasters are supposed to look, sound, and behave. This quickly crafted surface persona is usually pieced together with poor or misinformed choices and entrenched with bad habits. And although the mask they create is often devoid of the complexities a strong communication skill-set can offer for a sustainable career, by the time most of them are confronted with a talent coach, that surface persona has been galvanized onto their being. And because it got them this far in their career, they are dubious that enhancing it or replacing it will garner better results, and mistrustful of anyone who suggests otherwise.

What you may find surprising is that this book was born out of the fact that I absolutely love coaching anchors, reporters and weathercasters. Because once the hurdle of their uncertainty and mistrust is cleared, the potential for a great career by utilizing the following concepts and techniques in this book is unlimited. And taking that ride with them is exhilarating.

WHAT YOU WILL LEARN

The essential skill-set anchors, reporters and weathercasters must possess to be compelling and successful encompasses so much more than the ability to speak in front of a camera or group of people. Most of us can do that to some degree. It is about understanding and utilizing the concepts involved in mastering the art of powerful communication. You will learn the fundamental and vital techniques that support those concepts; born out of the human condition and supported by the dynamics of body language, voice, speech, storytelling, understanding an audience, ideal interactions, perspective, and even writing.

WHAT YOU WILL NEED

Since the teacher is only as good as the student, to fully process and utilize this information, you will need the willingness to experience new things outside of your comfort zone, the capacity to adapt and change with the times, the fortitude to rigorously prepare, and the determination to practice until it becomes second nature.

So, are you ready? Excellent. Let's go!

Chapter 1

VALUE BEYOND THE CONTENT

Your fate was set long before you hit the stage.
Winning is all about preparation. Period.

Mastering the art of powerful communication takes an understanding that mastery is a journey, not a destination. That, in fact, fervency of the journey is the goal, and being fully invested in present-time is the strongest way to travel on that path.

The broadcast news business, like any other, has its share of dilettantes. A dilettante is someone who cultivates an area of interest without real commitment. It is the student who can't find the time to pick up a book outside of the classroom. The artist who doesn't take the time to study technique. The athlete who doesn't pay attention to health and wellbeing off the field. The musician who doesn't practice or study theory. The news anchor who doesn't prep or practice. The performer who doesn't study craft or rehearse. The actor who doesn't fully commit to learning lines, being the character, studying the art... I can go on and on. And then these folks get confused as to why they aren't developing faster or having better success. Dilettantes tend to blame outside influences for not being prepared to be their best. Too often dilettantes will complain that their performance suffers because of bad relationships that get in the way of preparation or being in the right frame of mind. A dilettante thinks that the only time it's important to be truly invested is "when it counts." Which only goes to show that they don't understand the concept of "when it counts."

A dilettante doesn't understand that being the best is not about having the most talent. It's about having a technique so strong and so unwavering that it supports whatever talent is possessed, no matter the situation. As a master of the craft, it means that you will always perform at the top of your game no matter the size of audience or paycheck. Mastery in ANY high-profile profession is a life-long journey of developing that technique with ardent study and a training that is always pushing the professional a little closer to the sun.

The following pages were written with the assumption that you are already on the road to mastery. You may be just at the beginning of that journey. Or maybe you already have a career supported by a strong foundation. In that case, no one needs to tell you how to do your job because you already KNOW how to do your job. In fact, as far as you're concerned and your family and friends are concerned and even most of your viewers are concerned, you're pretty damn good at your job, thank you very much. You might even be considered by many to be the top dog in your pack.

But there is a catch. And it's probably the reason you started reading this book in the first place. It is a concern that brings to mind the African parable about the gazelle that wakes each morning thinking he must run faster than the fastest lion to survive the day. The lion by contrast thinks he must run faster than the slowest gazelle or he'll starve. In any case, no matter what role you play, when the sun comes up, you'd better be running. Running as fast as you can.

Even though everyone may tell you that you're skilled and talented and certainly good enough, you have this nagging feeling that it isn't enough. A concern skulking around in the dark corners of your psyche that the career you've so meticulously built and worked so hard to achieve, although (somewhat) fulfilling and (hopefully) lucrative, may not be all that stable. It is quite a fickle business, after all. And with all that confidence you show the world as you soldier on during the most uncertain time in the history of the broadcast news business, at your core you know damn well that success is never final. And because of this, there are two truisms that you've done your best not to contemplate, but that you know you will eventually have to face head-on:

1) **Nothing remains the same.**
   Things either get better or they get worse.

   - and -

2) **If you don't evolve, you WILL be overtaken.**
   Then passed over... then forgotten.

Yikes! And you thought this was going to be an uplifting read. It gets better, I promise.

WORK TAKES THE TIME ALLOTTED

I started working with broadcast news folks as a performance coach, writing coach, Camera Choreographer and Show Doctor in the mid 1980's. At that time, using a personal computer and the internet to drive a business was possible (sort of), but not really a thing. CNN had only been around for a few years with no real rival. Local news stations were just making a big push to automate their production systems and the use of robotic cameras was novel at best, and comically unreliable at times. In fact, every few months, another video-taped blooper reel would surface, making its way around the country showcasing some runaway robotic camera mowing down its floor crew and anchors. Fun times! (Interesting to note that the first Terminator movie came out at about the same time as those homicidal cameras were on the loose. Coincidence? I don't think so.) And when I say, "make its way around the country," please remember that, at the time, there was no 'world-wide web.' An actual person had to physically travel with and deliver that bloopers VHS or BETA tape or it had to be FedExed for others to enjoy. So, to go to all that trouble, the contents on that cassette tape had to be some funny s*$#t!

During those ancient times, there were still directors and camera operators who were trained in the cinematic arts. Producers took pride in crafting their stories, checking their facts for accuracy and their writing for proper grammar and spelling. (I know, right?!?) Opinion Journalism were two words you would NEVER see in the same sentence much less together. And anchors had the time necessary before every show to prep their scripts as storytellers and during the show to interpret and deliver that copy so that they came across to the audience as commanding and conversational. This was especially important because viewers watched local news (and still do) for three very simple reasons:

VIEWERS WATCH THE LOCAL NEWS TO...
- ✓ Help them protect their families.
- ✓ Help their families live better in the community.
- ✓ Help them to enhance their family's lives.

Therefore, viewers wanted (and still do) on-camera personalities to embrace their sensibilities because they were under the romantic (but very false) presumption that the anchors ran the ship. They assumed (and still do) that the anchors wrote, produced, edited, directed and assigned the stories that would be on the air. So viewers figured that, if they chose to watch on-camera personalities that were just like them, then the show's content would be tailor-made just for them. Logical. Right?

Of course, that doesn't mean everyone working behind and in front of the cameras actually took the time to do their jobs to the best of their abilities, or even that everyone had the same skill set or talents necessary to do so. Which is why I was never out of a job. Keeping news folks on track, tweaking their skills, and teaching newbies how to be as diligent with the craft as those who came before them. That was coaching… then.

Today, local and cable news outlets are a whole different breed. On this digitally automated computerized web-driven 24/7 news cycle planet, they must constantly feed the same content in different ways to multiple radio and TV channels, platforms, and social media sites. And with less staffers to do all of that feeding, producing the news has become less about connecting with the viewers (no time for that) and more about churning out as much product as quickly as possible. There's an old adage that goes, "Work takes the time allotted." Remember in school when they gave you a week to write a paper, that it would take you about a week to accomplish the task? However, if they only gave you three days, then it would only take about three days. And if they only gave you an hour to turn in that same assignment, then it would only take you about an hour. Many newsrooms today seem to run on this 'work takes the time allotted' concept. So the time that used to be given to write, produce and perform a show has been cut dramatically, assuming the same results can still be achieved, merely by the asking.

Unfortunately, to produce product that quickly, floor crews have become an endangered species making way for robotics. Seasoned directors who crafted artistic ways to shoot and pace shows have been replaced by 'technical directors' who spend most of their time 'coding' shows. (Typing shorthand language [code] into a computer so that the robotic cameras know where to move and when.) Fewer producers staff the newsroom, hired not for their creative writing skills but rather the speed in which they are able to cut-and-paste content from one platform into the next. (This is one reason there seems to be so much redundancy between shows. If you've seen the 5am, there's no need to stick around for the 6am since it'll be much the same content communicated in much the same way.) And if you see your anchors verbally stumbling on camera, it's most likely due to the fact that before the show they were so busy answering emails, posting on social media sites, and fixing spelling, grammatical errors and fact checking, that they didn't have time to look at all of their scripts, much less decide how they would deliver them, and are reading them cold, for the first time, to you, on the air. Eek.

THE HUMAN CONDITION

Please understand me when I say that I'm not criticizing these folks in the least. Most are well intended, hard-working employees doing the jobs that they've been given to do, to the best of their abilities. The problem is, although technology has changed the way news is produced and distributed, and corporations have figured out how to squeeze as much content as possible out of the least number of employees in the shortest amount of time, something very important is being lost in the process. It's the very thing that drove human beings to want that content 30 years ago and 300 years ago and 30,000 years ago. And it is the same thing that drives them today. People crave THE

HUMAN CONDITION. In fact, as a rule, people don't care about data without the human condition attached to it.

THE HUMAN CONDITION

1) *The totality of human behavioral patterns, ideas and attitudes.*

2) *Life's events and encounters that are susceptible to or representative of a human beings' sympathies, passions, and feelings.*

3) *The conscious understanding of good and evil, spirit and mortality.*

Love, hate, anger, fear, jealousy, hunger… most of us have the same understanding of these states and the same reality on them, so they are considered human conditions. The human condition can also be attached to ideas and things. If you ask a hundred people to comment on a picture of a rock, you'll get many different answers because there is no single human condition connected to a rock. However, if you ask that same group of folks to comment on a picture of a baby that has been badly beaten, you'll get a similar kind of response from just about everyone, because there's a real human condition attached to that kind of image.

A robbery means very little to your audience until they know the circumstance. Three middle-aged men knocking over a downtown ATM in the middle of the night will illicit a very different response from viewers than three teenaged boys robbing an old lady on a Sunday in the middle of the park. The prospect of five inches of rain means something very different to a viewer living on a flood plain as it does to someone living in a drought. And what of killing an animal? If someone shoots a rabid bobcat that was about to murder your child, you'd probably be okay with that. On the other hand, if he shot your child's pet kitten for sport, maybe not so much. In each case, it's not about the thing that happened (robbery, weather condition, killing), it's about the human conditions surrounding or attached to that incident that actually compels viewers and connects them to that information. People relate better to the information, have more affinity for the story, and will remember the story's details longer when it is intertwined with the human condition. And the natural inclination is to gravitate towards stories offering the strongest human conditions.

Understanding the human condition as a concept and mastering its use is paramount because a high story count, a pretty set, and a clean show without technical gaffs may be desirable goals, but attaining them will not significantly grow your audience or your career. As an anchor, reporter, or weathercaster, if you cannot find a way to consistently weave the human condition into your work, your chances of success greatly diminish as the chances for your competition's success multiply, whether that competition is across the street or in your own shop.

VALUE BEYOND THE CONTENT

The concepts in this book are based on enduring and immutable human condition principles that have stood the test of time. There are basic doctrines that have been the cornerstones of my teachings for over three decades. One of which is that the human condition should always be at the core of a storyteller's presentation. Another is that, a professional who wants long-term career success must perform and deliver in such a way as to become valuable to the viewers beyond the content. That's right, I said it!

To ensure your career success…
BE VALUABLE BEYOND THE CONTENT!!

Blasphemy! I know, I know.

"Bill! What about the enduring tried-and-true Journalism adage that Content is King?!?"

"Well, it is… until it isn't."

Yes, viewers want great content. They would rather it be Shakespeare than schlock. On the other hand, I've seen some pretty bad actors attempt Shakespeare and, guess what, it ain't Shakespeare anymore. It sucks. Yes, Shakespeare in the wrong hands SUCKS! On top of that, in today's world audiences know that they can get that content from myriad sources. So why choose you? They will choose you because you've made yourself **valuable beyond the content.**

Viewers will choose you and be loyal to you because your body language, your variations of tone, your vocal variety, the words you use and how you use them, your storytelling skills, your confidence and consistency are not only compelling, but they work together to impress upon viewers that you care about them and that you are there for their well-being and to keep them safe. They will be assured that you will help them protect their family, live better in their community and enhance their lives. And if you're good, really good, consistently good, viewers will want to watch you every day, regardless of that day's news content or the weather conditions.

Understanding how and why these concepts work and gaining the skills to consistently produce them so that you are valuable beyond the content… that is what this book is all about.

YOU DIDN'T EAT THE TAIL?

Many restaurants fall by the wayside because they operate under the assumption that providing good food is enough to stay in business. Successful restaurants know that, although the food is important, it is only one of many necessary elements in the whole dining experience. The big picture, the overriding goal, isn't to just serve decent food; it's to get the patron to return. That means great service, atmosphere, cleanliness, legible menus, the server's demeanor, etc. Making the whole experience a great experience is how a restaurant, or any business, stays in business. With television news, delivering the data is no different than delivering food to the patron. Conversational storytelling, open throws, human condition leads and tags, perspective, substantive interactions, etc., are just some of the elements that help to make a newscast a 'four-star' experience.

There is an old Greek expression I learned from my grandmother when I was a kid. She spoke very little English and loved to pass on her wisdom through sayings and maxims recorded all the way back to the Golden Age of Greece. One of her favorites was, *"Trógate to gáidaro kai giatí afínete tin ourá?"* Loosely translated, "You ate the whole jackass but you left the tail?!?" I know, I know. She was from 'the old country,' what can I say. Anyway, the saying actually makes sense and is humorous if you know the language. It's a comment on someone who goes to all the trouble of doing a thing, completes all the tough stuff related to that thing, but leaves out the easiest part, so that in the end, although the job is technically 'done,' it isn't really fully done.

All that to say, if you're going to read this book, do yourself a favor and read the whole book. Although there are chapters devoted to specific talents, i.e. Anchors, Reporters, and

Weathercasters, every chapter has information that will help you to achieve value beyond the content, no matter your expertise.

Chapter 2

"THE TALENT"

Talent without technique is a tail wagging the dog.

Okay. I get it. You're talented. You grew up knowing that you're talented. You got acceptance and applause and love because of it. You're one of the few lucky ones because you were born with it. Just a bit brighter or faster or stronger or prettier or wittier than the rest of us. Birds sing when you walk by. And you smell like freshly baked cookies. Seriously, I get it.

And if that's all that it took to become successful, you would probably already be a rock star. Unfortunately for you, most of the folks that stand on your side of the camera are ALSO talented. They are also a bit shinier. Also with the birds and the cookies. So, what's the secret? What elevates one talent above the rest into a super stratosphere that few reach and everyone covets? Over the years I've come to find that the superstars who dominate this field seem to operate under a set core beliefs that drives their careers. One of those overriding maxims is this:

Preparation is 90% of the game.

Earthshattering? Of course not. There's probably not much I'm going to tell you in this book that will surprise you. What is surprising, however, are the number of professionals who know this is a huge factor for success and still don't adhere to it. I've often said that the news business is the only high-profile profession that doesn't prep, practice or rehearse. What professional athlete tells the coach, "I don't need to practice, just put me in the game!" What brain surgeon says, "Just bring me the brain, I read about the procedure. Let's just see how it goes!" Eighty-seven percent of an athlete's career is practice. Doctors and lawyers are required to take continuing education courses. Corporations put their managers and staffs through leadership workshops and seminars. Singers and dancers and actors take classes or study their parts or rehearse before every gig. But every day on every show, anchors and reporters will jump in front of a camera without warming up, reading the copy out loud, considering how they are going to interpret that copy, or even having a strong understanding of their target viewer. Then, after it's all said and done, few look at the finished product to study and adjust for any mistakes or just a better way to perform the next go-around. Then everyone wonders why folks in this business don't get better faster or why they keep stumbling or why they're not building a career as quickly as they'd like. Seriously?!?

I'm currently working with an NFL linebacker who wants to get better with his public speaking skills. Before our first session I had the priceless opportunity to watch as he practiced with his team for an upcoming game. When we finally met a few days later, I commented on how grueling the practice looked and said to him offhandedly, "You've got to hate practice!"

"No, I love practice." he said, quite seriously.

"Really?" I'm thinking, why would anyone put themselves thru that kind of torture unless they're getting paid. A LOT. Which, of course, he is. So, I pushed on.

"Why?"

"Because it's the only time I get to fall on my butt." he said.

That threw me. "And why do you want to fall on your butt?"

He looked at me as if I had just asked where babies come from.

"Because it's the only time you learn anything." he said.

I looked at him as if I still didn't understand where babies come from, so he continued.

"During a game," he said, "I can't screw around and try out new things. I've got to stay in my lane 'cause I got mouths to feed."

Now this guy's "lane" is pretty big. He's been playing ball for fifteen years and there aren't many players out there who are at his level.

"But if I stay in my lane for too long," he continued, "there's gonna be another guy who's younger or hungrier or prettier…" then he took a beat, smiled and shook his head as if to jokingly say no one could be prettier, then continued, "and eventually he's gonna pass me. And then those mouths I've been feedin' are gonna go hungry."

And it all fell into place.

"And you don't learn anything if you're always playing it safe," I said.

His smile broadened, "That's right! That's right! My man!"

Many times, when I suggest to broadcast news clients that they prep, practice, or rehearse, they look at me like I don't know where babies come from, because in their minds, what I'm suggesting is that they're not talented enough or that they don't know their business or that they're not good at what they do. And that just isn't the case. Practice is all about tweaking and honing the skills already learned and pushing talent to find more dynamic ways of expression. There's an old Zen saying which goes something like this:

**"If you hit the bull's eye every time,
you're standing too close to the target!"**
Some Zen guy.

This is true of any perishable skill. (And trust me when I say, the broadcast news profession is built on perishable skills.) If you've been in the business for any length of time, you are well aware that, like Sisyphus rolling the same bolder up the same mountain day-after-day, you're covering the same kinds of stories, writing the same kinds of copy, and building the same kinds of segments. And human nature dictates that repetition eventually softens the edge, kills urgency and causes aptitude to falter. It's just the way of things. To keep things fresh, there are specific pre-show check lists that are unique to the anchor, reporter or weathercaster that we will discuss in each of their chapters. But for now, let's look at the preparations that should be elemental for every on-camera personality.

✓ **Self-worth and professional consistency go hand-in-hand.** The great acting coaching Stanislavski once wrote that becoming a great actor meant working on 'the self' as much as working on the part. It is vital to understand that confidence in your body, spirit and mind translates to the work. Asserting that you have no time to eat properly, exercise or feed your soul is tantamount to a declaration that you have no time for a long-lasting successful career. You don't make chairs for a living. YOU are your living! So, if you care about that living, you take care of yourself.

✓ **REHEARSE!** If you've ever thought to yourself right after a performance that you could have done it better with a second take, chances are you didn't rehearse it. Physically RUN THRU IT out loud and in real time before the show! I know running thru a 1 to 3-minute piece seems like a lifetime to you, but it's only 1 to 3-minutes! I now have client stations that actually run through the entire first block of a show just before air to work out all the kinks. As a result, they springboard into their shows with more confidence and pop… and virtually no glitches.

✓ **Wipe your feet at the door**. We all have a life with problems, none of which that can be resolved during a show. Since consistency is a key for success, superstars know how to disengage from their 'real-life' issues before each show so that the performance is always pure. Many have pre-show rituals that aid in the process. Some meditate, others do calisthenics. Take five minutes to calm, and focus the mind on who you need to be for the next hour, who your target viewer is, what motivated you to get into this business in the first place, pumping yourself up with investment, etc. It may sound cheesy or hokey to you, but it works. So, do it!

✓ **Back-time your day**. If you start your day with the knowledge that you have up until seconds before air to do everything else you normally do, sans taking time to rehearse and focus, then you will never have the time to rehearse or focus. If you walk into your day deciding that you must complete all your assignments with enough time to rehearse and focus, those things are more likely to happen. I know that it's 'news' and things come up at the last minute. However, 'back-timing' is a great way to hedge your bets.

✓ **Review airchecks**. Everyone needs a dispassionate third-eye to monitor progress and push for adjustments and growth. Unfortunately, unless you have your own private coach that's looking after you on a daily basis, that dispassionate third-eye is going to have to be YOU! At least once each week, review an aircheck of your work. You will watch it at least twice. Once with the audio turned off so that you can concentrate on body language, facial expressions, hair, make-up, clothing choices, deportment, etc. On the second pass, turn the audio up and close your eyes or turn away from the screen so that you only focus on your vocal quality, vocal variety, conversational quality, and word choice. You'll find reviewing airchecks in this fashion to be more revealing and helpful because it will allow you to be more objective.

✓ **Party with a purpose.** It's hard to hit a target you can't see. So, to assure a stellar party, you begin with a vision. Date, location, theme, number of guests, kinds of food, etc. Once you have that plan, you can execute accordingly. Simple, right? Now we all know that plans rarely come to fruition without a hitch. But it's also important to note that having a plan will usually get you closer to the intended mark. The same can be said for your performance, your show and your career. It's never going to go exactly as planned. But working toward a vision is always more productive than the 'let's just see what comes' attitude. Highly successful people are list makers. Lists for the day, the project, the week, the month, the year, and so on. As they go and priorities change, those lists are modified and the final goals are redefined. But make no mistake about it, they never would have reached those modified goals had they not gotten on the path to begin with. A path that began with a list.

PERSONALITY ISN'T A DIRTY WORD

Many on-camera news folks and "Capital 'J' Journalists" (a very serious bunch) cringe when they hear the word "personality" because they associate it with being overly happy or exuberant to the point of insincerity or annoyance. And who wants that? Especially if they're covering a hard news story. However, if you do a little research on the word, you'll find that personality doesn't mean, "happy."

per·son·al·i·ty [pùrss'n állətee]

1) A person's set of characteristics: the totality of a person's attitudes, interests, behavioral patterns, emotional responses, social roles, and other individual traits that endure over long periods of time.

2) Characteristics making a person appealing; the distinctive or very noticeable characteristics that make a person socially appealing.

3) Somebody regarded as epitomizing traits: somebody regarded as epitomizing particular character traits.

So, when I say that you need 'personality' infused into your work, what I'm suggesting is that you utilize the totality of characteristics and sensibilities that make up a human being's character and that connect to all the basic human conditions in life. An on-camera communicator with "personality" is one that is invested, conversational, approachable, strong, energized, and attaches the appropriate emotional tones to the words and stories that connect on a human level with the viewer. No matter the content or tone of the story being told, viewers want the person telling it to have 'personality.' This helps viewers to process the information and to have an emotional connection to the story. It also allows them to connect to the communicator on a more personal level, which is important if you want the viewer's loyalty, not just their immediate attention. Your ability to infuse personality into presentations is one of the few advantages you have when the audience is deciding to listen to you versus reading those same stories from the internet.

ATTITUDE ADJUSTMENTS

I'm sure we can all agree that attitude goes a long way toward making or breaking a career. This book is filled with techniques that, if mastered, will brilliantly showcase talent. However, if the attitude driving that technique is poor, then the talent never seems to manifest the strength and power needed to reach its potential. So, when you need to pop that attitude into high-gear, or you just need a little attitude adjustment, here are a few maxims I've penned over the years to help.

> ➤ **The Subconscious is a powerful thing!**

> > ○ *It does what you tell it!* Say out loud, "I can't afford it," and your subconscious will keep you from that money. Lie to everyone that you're not feeling well, and your subconscious will give you those symptoms. Say, "I can't do it," and it will keep you from that ability. Criticize another's good fortune, and your subconscious will keep good fortune just out of your reach.

> > ○ *It doesn't like avoidance.* When you think to yourself, "Don't hit the wall!" your subconscious hears, "Hit the wall… hard!" Don't confuse your subconscious. Tell it what you want, not what you don't want.

> > ○ *Eradicate your lexicon of phrases like, "I can't," "I'm not," or, "It's a problem."* When speaking to others or to yourself, feed your subconscious positive messages to act on like, "I can," "I will," and, "There's a solution!"

○ *It will mold you into the character you tell others you have.* Speak with malice or evil intent and your subconscious will convert your being to reflect those words. Tell others you are here to raise the spirit of mankind, and the same will apply. So be positive when speaking, because your subconscious is listening.

➢ **Don't let the perfect be the enemy of the good.** Those who need perfection to feel actualized will always fail because perfection doesn't exist. Make every effort to be the best! Enjoy the process, always invest 110%, and be consistent with striving for a great performance, not a perfect one. If you're worried about mucking things up, you will. Ultimately, you won't be judged for making mistakes. Everyone makes mistakes. You will be judged for how you handle mistakes when they happen. You know how to do your job and you do it well. Trust your training, be in present time and look toward the future.

➢ **Be assertive without being aggressive**. There are three kinds of behavior that people demonstrate in their professional and personal lives: Passive, Aggressive and Assertive.

○ **Passive people** achieve little while allowing others to violate their rights.

○ **Aggressive people** achieve their goals while violating the rights of others.

○ **Assertive people** achieve their goals while doing their best not to violate the rights of others. In fact, they create an atmosphere for everyone around them to win as well.

An assertive person will say, "This is my ship and it's going in this direction. Now you have a choice. You can get on my ship. You can follow my ship. You can go in another direction on your own. Or you can lead my ship." In all cases, the assertive person creates an environment where everyone has the opportunity and ability to win.

Except for one. The one thing an assertive person will not allow is for someone to divert or impede the ship. The assertive person will say, "I want you to succeed, and I will give you every opportunity to do so. However, if you get in front of my ship and stop, well... it's a ship. And it will run you over."

Although aggressive people have been known to succeed, I always suggest that the best choice for an extended run of success is to adopt the style of the assertive person. It takes a certain kind of energy and mind set, but it is a style that I believe is much more sustainable.

➢ **Drive the car!** It surprising the number of times I have to work with folks to build up their confidence because, down deep inside, they don't feel worthy of the position they've been given. Here's the deal... you wanted the job, you GOT the job, now, DO THE JOB! If someone gives you the keys to their car, even though it isn't YOUR car, you still need to drive with the confidence that you OWN IT. If you don't, they'll want those keys back and they won't want to give you another chance to drive. So, DRIVE!

➢ **Behavior Modification.** Do a thing long enough and you become that thing. Decide what kind of talent you want to be; commanding, gracious, perspective driven, viewer centric, etc. Write all the characteristics down then mentally go through your show to determine when and how you can exhibit those traits.   Over time the mechanics of performing those characteristics will become second nature and you will be the very thing you've been performing.   This is how a profession becomes an identifiable persona and overwhelming career force.

Chapter 3

THE EYES HAVE IT

Visualize what you want to realize!
Goals are like targets.
To hit them, you have to SEE them.

The video screen, whether it's on your TV, computer, or smart phone, is one of the most powerful communicators on our planet. This is because the strongest element of communication is the visual image. It's just the way the brain works. It works visually first. More than half of communication is based on what we see or what we can get others to see. To understand a concept, remember it, or to refer to it, the mind will first try to attach an image to that concept. Right now, if I tell you that your best friend is driving around in a red drop-top Cadillac, you wouldn't immediately begin to spell out R-E-D C-A-D-I-L-L-A-C in your mind. Instead, your brain would conjure up an image (if it hasn't already) of what it perceives your friend would look like driving that car. If you had never seen a Cadillac before, your brain would do its best to pull from the lifetime collection of images it has on other cars, along with my verbal description, to create a visual point of reference.

Visual impressions do more to facilitate our understanding and memory retention than do the other senses. The massive stock pile of visual images in your brain is constantly being referenced as an initial decision maker. Therefore, the visual image will always trump the audio. In other words, people will always believe what they see over what they hear. If a guy is shaking his head 'no' while telling you to trust him, you're not going to trust him no matter how convincing his voice may sound, because his visual message is telling you, "NOOOOO!" How many times do you see people for the first time and before they say a word, you already have an opinion about them?   Just by looking at them?! Or a quick glance gives you all the information you feel you need to decide their background, social status, personality, even sexual orientation. All before they open their mouth. And after speaking with them, you still hold tightly to your preconceptions even though what they say, their voices or speech patterns seem to communicate a different impression. The visual image is so strong the brain will want to believe what it sees over anything else it senses.

Success in this business means that you understand the power of visual elements and utilize them to initiate the best first impressions, feelings and style. Body language, hair, make-up, clothes, how viewers see you deal with the environment, how they see you deal with other people… these are all extremely important because they guide the viewers perceptions of who you are, if you are to be listened to, and if you are to be trusted.

It's not about being 'pretty.' It's not about looking like you just stepped out of a glamour magazine. We're not doing *Entertainment Tonight*; we're doing the news! (Of course, if we were doing *ET*, it would most certainly be about your face, body, hair, make-up and jewelry!) Although being attractive doesn't hurt, in the news game it's all about the visual image coming across as appropriate. Looking and acting the part. You wouldn't want your doctor walking in for your exam wearing a clown outfit. Even with great references, high-achievement awards and a fantastic staff, the red nose and floppy shoes would certainly send you running out of the medical office in a fight-or-flight panic. It's much the same for the news game. If you don't visually look and act like the viewers' perception of your job, then they will think you're not all that good at your job, no matter the reality.

APPROACHABILITY AND STRENGTH

To be a solid anchor, reporter or weathercaster, the viewers want you to have a balance of approachability and strength. On the one hand, they want to feel like they could walk up to you on the street and be comfortable introducing themselves and their families and chatting about the day's events. On the other hand, they want to feel like if there are wolves at their doors, you'll handle it. That you'll take care of any situation and that you'll protect them. I've seen that word a lot in research project verbatims over the years: "Protector." Viewers want to know that you're looking out for them. That you'll protect them.

Later in the book we'll talk about various ways to convey approachability and strength through the voice, the words that you use and the way that you deliver those words. But for now, let's look at the opportunities you have to demonstrate those elements visually.

BODY LANGUAGE

The more you know about the subtle nonverbal cues we send to each other, the better you will become as a communicator. Since there are literally thousands of books that have been written about the intricacies of body language, detailing everything from micro-expressions to positioning to kinetics, I won't attempt a comprehensive discussion here. However, over the years I've found that there are certain body language tools and techniques that are vital when performing in front of the camera to insure approachability and strength.

THE HANDS

The hands can be a very powerful communicator or a very annoying distraction. Some things to keep in mind:

➢ **It is important to use them to communicate when appropriate.** Imagine if I asked you to sit on your hands and then tell me a funny story. It would be hard to do. Sitting on your hands would lock up your shoulders, which in turn would lock up your neck and then your facial expressions, which would stifle your vocal variety. When used appropriately, the hands open your expressiveness potential and offer visual cues that allow the audience to follow along.

➢ **Keep them in the 'Neutral Zone.'** The Neutral Zone is that area between your waist and your chest. When your hands are in the Neutral Zone and moving naturally, they are the least distracting and can be the most effective. Never put them behind you or in your pockets or clasped below your waist.

➢ **When standing**: you can allow your hands the freedom of movement to support your communication, you can put them by your sides, or you can lightly touch them together just above the waist (being careful not to form them into a geometric shape). If you use them to communicate, keep them in that 'neutral zone' above your waist and below your chest so that they don't become distracting. Again, avoid clasping your hands or idly fiddling with your fingers, as that can be distracting to the viewer.

➢ **Drop those scripts and I-Pads whenever possible.** The need to hold scripts and/or devices is understandable when there is a lot of mobility during the show or the prompter

(prompter operator) has the tendency of doing what it wants when it wants. However, keep in mind that scripts and I-Pads are a big distraction to the viewer and holding them tends to stifle vocal expression and variety. Hold them when you must, but drop them when you can.

➢ **Stay open when sitting at a desk.** Avoid clasping or fidgeting with your hands in front of you or playing with pens and scripts. In addition to hindering your expressiveness potential, clasped hands look defensive and provide an obstacle between you and the viewer. And shuffling scripts or twirling pens is just plain distracting.

➢ **Keep hand gestures outside of your body**. This goes equally when standing or when sitting at the desk. Keeping your hand gestures outside of your body creates a more dynamic message and the perception that you have a strong demeanor.

➢ **Square up your shoulders in single-shots.** Many times, I'll see anchors with their shoulders at a slight angle during their tight-shots. Consider the camera as being a single viewer. If you were conversing with that viewer face-to-face in real time, you wouldn't be standing at an angle, looking at her over one shoulder. That would just be weird and distracting. Right? If you want that person to like you and respect you, square up!

➢ **Don't let the tail wag the dog**. Excessive body language, shuffling or swaying while standing is distracting and weakens the message. Also, if you are in perpetual motion, any movement you intend to make for emphasis will be diluted. Focus that energy into vocal variety and hand gestures within the neutral zone. Only move when there is a reason to move.

> **A one-quarter (or 'First Position') stance at the monitor or in front of the key is strong and probably the most versatile.** Your delivery will be stronger if you can stay somewhat open to the viewer as well as the monitor/key during the entire presentation. A one-quarter stance allows you to indicate what's in the monitor/key while still being open to the viewer.

> **Avoid repetitive gestures.** Repetitive movement isn't normal during social interactions and can appear robotic, stiff or 'cold' on camera. It is extremely important to utilize body language as a support for your message, but it is equally important to vary those gestures so that you come across as relaxed and conversational.

> **Really pull something off that script.** If you use the convention of looking down at your script as a transition between stories, make sure it looks like you are actually reading a phrase or even a word to springboard you into the next story. Otherwise it can come across as by wrote or insincere.

> **Practice strong eye contact.** Look at the anchors or look at the viewer. Rarely should you look down unless you want to show that you are reading something directly from copy to give the fact credence. Otherwise, looking down can come across as 'shifty' or unsure.

> **Have good and relaxed posture at the desk!** Sit comfortably, but straight. Imagine a string attached to the top of your head gently pulling you toward the ceiling.

Make sure those shoulders aren't scrunched up around your neck. And there should be little or no weight placed on your forearms. Keep those arms open and those hands unclenched.

➤ **Position your body so that you look like a strong team.** During 2-shots with your co-anchor you should be turned slightly so that it appears you are open to both your co-anchor and to the viewer.

➤ **While sitting at a desk, keep those elbows level or above the tabletop.** When the elbows are below the plane of the tabletop, the angle of the arms forces the anchor to put weight on the desk with the forearms, hindering movement and giving the appearance that the anchor isn't big enough to be sitting there. Elbows above the plane of the tabletop allow a freer range of movement and give the appearance that the anchor is in command of the surrounding real estate.

➤ **Facial expressions.** Review a few airchecks by turning off the audio and just watching. Proper facial expressions should help the viewer to track emotional variations in stories, and transitions between one story and the next. Monitor yourself for those expressions during your aircheck reviews. Work on developing a wider range of facial expressions to highlight emotional tones and transitions.

WARDROBE

You don't have a second chance to make a good first impression. Think of your clothes, make-up, hair and jewelry as if they were the frame of a painting. When you go to a museum and look at a painting, if your first thought is, "Great frame!" then it's a lousy frame. No matter how ornate and expensive, the frame is supposed to make you look at the painting, not detract from it. Similarly, your wardrobe is supposed to direct the viewer to focus on your face and what you are saying, not detract from it.

> **Find your look and perfect it!** There are myriad factors that dictate what looks best on you and what you look best in. I'm not a stylist and truly respect the ones who understand that it's not just about the name brands you make-up with or wear . Getting your look 'right' means having an understanding about your skin tone, facial structure and body type. It means knowing who your target viewer is and the latest fashion trends in your market as well as in the country that she (the viewer) deems approachable, strong and appropriate.

But there's more! If a stylist promises you the perfect look by rifling thru your closet for the perfect outfits and giving you a make-up tutorial in front of your own bathroom mirror for the perfect complexion, all without ever setting foot in your station's studio... run. Seriously, RUN!

Great stylists understand that environment must be a major consideration when choosing colors, clothing and make-up. And if they are really seasoned, they'll know that different studios will change the way you look and the way those things look on you because of factors like set colors, lighting hues, lighting types (Quartz, Fresnel, LED, etc.) and the types and ages of the studio's cameras.

Certainly, there are general cardinal rules to keep in mind:

- o Avoid busy patterns, flashy jewelry, high-shine lip gloss and hot colors.

- o Cool colors and jewel tones seem to work better for most folks.

- o Avoid wearing colors that blend into the set. The idea is that you want to 'pop' when in front of the set.

- o Avoid all white, green and yellow outfits.

- o Match the make-up on the Décolletage (neck and upper chest) with the face.

Having said all of that, I know that most of you don't have the luxury of working with a stylist, so the most important thing is to monitor yourself by testing looks on camera or reviewing airchecks to see what works best for you. Occasional wardrobe and makeup 'malfunctions' are recoverable. But consistent faux paus can seriously hinder a career. Remember, it's a visual medium. So be vigilant here.

A WORD ABOUT HAIR

Hair styles for female anchors have changed dramatically over the years. In the late '80's and early 90's they were mostly tame and 'professional'. With the advent of cable news, style choices have become much more about 'sex appeal.' As I said, I am not a stylist, so I won't profess to know how long your extensions should be at any given time. But I do know this. If your hair covers up or partly obscures your eye(s) or eyebrow(s), it's going to be distracting and annoying to the viewer. This isn't my opinion. It's a fact borne out by hundreds of research projects over the past 30 years.   At the risk of sounding like a schoolmaster…

KEEP YOUR HAIR OUT OF YOUR EYES!

Ridiculous request, right? Of course, you wouldn't hide your eyes! But I'm not just talking about your single shots looking straight into the camera. I'm also talking about 2-shots and group shots when you're looking at co-anchors and we're faced with your profile. In many of these cases, we can't see your eyes because of those… uh, 'stylish' bangs.

Chapter 4

IT'S ALL ABOUT MARIA

There is no key to success.
But the key to failure is trying to make everyone like you.

To be successful as an anchor, reporter or weathercaster, it is incumbent on you to be an extraordinary storyteller. That much we know. What most journalists and meteorologists don't know when they start out in this business is that great storytelling is not about the subject matter and it's not about the story's structure. Two people could tell you the same exact story and you might love one and hate the other. On top of that, it's very likely you would walk away with two completely different experiences and feelings about that information.

And let's face it, when it comes right down to it, there are only a limited number of stories on the planet, anyway. We just keep finding different ways to tell them over-and-over again. The *David and Goliath* story is also the *Rocky* story. *Romeo and Juliet* is *West Side Story*. And the current political situation in our country is *Much Ado About Nothing*. Or *Apocalypse Now*. I still haven't decided.

Don't get me wrong. Subject matter and structure are important for the master communicator. If you want to be a great cook, you should have a comprehensive knowledge of basic ingredients and how they work together to create a meal. If you want a strong understanding of how most of our greatest stories in books and movies are structured, a blueprint for storytelling if you will, you should read Joseph Campbell's book, *The Hero with a*

Thousand Faces. It discusses his theory that mythological stories from a great many cultures throughout history follow the same structure. This "hero's journey" is broken down into eleven stages:

1) The Call to Adventure
2) Refusal of the Call
3) Meeting the Mentor
4) Crossing the Threshold
5) Tests
6) Approaching the innermost Cave
7) Ordeal
8) Reward/Bliss
9) The Road Back
10) Resurrection
11) Master of Two Worlds

Sounds like every action/adventure movie in the Marvel Universe! As a matter of fact, George Lucas credits Campbell's book as influencing his *Star Wars* films. Another book you should be familiar with as a storyteller is Christopher Booker's *The Seven Basic Plots* which suggests that any story you hear follows one of (or a combination of) seven scenarios;

1) Rags to Riches
2) The Quest
3) Voyage and Return
4) Comedy
5) Tragedy
6) Rebirth
7) Overcoming the Monster

I'm thinking the first block of most news shows is dominated by number five. And the politics in our country... number seven.

The point is this; there's nothing new. There isn't anything you're going to tell viewers they haven't already heard before in one form or another. Fires, shootings, car wrecks, burglaries... we just keep churning out the same content, day-after-day. So why do viewers continue to listen? We've already discussed why they want the content (to enhance their lives, protect their families, and live better in the community). But they have countless sources for that content. The question becomes, why would they to want to receive that daily content from you?

THE SECRET OF LIFE

Great storytellers know that every story they tell is only about one thing... the listener. It's not about the storyteller and it's not about the story. It's about getting the listener to react to that story. It's about constructing it and telling in such a way that the viewer is compelled to listen.

We all have a family story we've told a hundred times. But each time we tell it we'll first decide if we need to change it up for the listener's benefit because every listener processes information differently. For a child you might use simpler language. For a best friend you might use an inside joke that only the two of you would know to illustrate a point. For a stranger you might leave out any profanity. For your golfing buddies or 'girls' night out' you might decide that gratuitous profanity is the only way to keep their attention. Storytelling is not about the story. It's about telling that story in a way that is most compelling for the listener. And make no mistake about it, today's radio and TV audiences will no longer settle for good reporters. What they want are GREAT storytellers!

Reporting versus Storytelling...

➢ **The Reporter:** Communicates facts in a linier, dispassionate manner, ensuring that the audience receives the information with a logical sensibility that reveals no bias or intent.

➢ **The Storyteller:** Finds the human condition of the story and makes it the core of that story, leading with heart and attaching emotional tones to the words and phrases that have the human condition throughout the piece to create a bigger bandwidth of emotion with its delivery. Without necessarily showing bias, great storytelling allows the audience to experience the breadth of the piece through vocal variety, body language, conversational writing, and human condition sensibilities.

I have been employed to coach a number of talk shows over the years because of what the networks or studios or production companies deemed as "a host problem." Maybe the ratings weren't quite where they should be or a research project demonstrated that the target demographic (the specific audience or consumer group stations and networks gear their shows towards, based mainly on age, gender and income) saw the host as awkward or annoying or a reason NOT to watch. And the next thing you know, I'm sitting in the Executive Producer's office having basically the same meeting I've had dozens of times before with dozens of different production companies for a wide variety of talk shows.

A long beat as the EP stares at me, deciding whether I'm up for the job.

"We have a host problem," she says.

"What's the problem, exactly?" I ask.

"Women don't like our host," she says.

"That is a problem," I nod in agreement.

Her face becomes stern, as if I'm not grasping the gravity of the situation.

"We need women to like this guy," she says, emphasizing the word "like."

"Yeah, I get that."

Since this isn't my first rodeo, I move the conversation along to where I know it's eventually going to have to go.

"Are you sure that it's only your host?" I ask.

"We only have one. Who else would it be?" Exasperated, "You have done this before, right?"

"What I mean to say is, sometimes the way monologues are written or the types of sketches he does or even the way a show is shot can alter the viewer's perception of the host."

She looks at me as if I've just made up a new language. She measures out her words to make them easier for me to understand.

"We... have... a... HOST... problem."

Of course, after reviewing airchecks or watching a live taping, what I'll find is that, although the host certainly needs to develop better skills and stronger techniques, there is usually a much larger issue, because hosts don't work in a vacuum. The way the show is written, produced, dressed and shot has a great deal to do with how the host, and the show is perceived. And all of that usually starts in the development stage when the producers and talent decided to create a show based on what THEY like in terms of the look, style, humor, and content, neglecting to consider that the target audience's sensibilities might be different from their own.

The mistake is a common one. Whether creating a show or preparing a speech, most folks begin by considering themselves first. If THEY were the audience what would THEY like to see and hear. What would THEY find interesting or funny. This kind of thinking can be the kiss of death, because the producers and writers are NOT the audience. Many times, they are not even close to the demographic and so they don't have the target viewer's sensibilities. In news, I've always found it fascinating that the target viewer is usually in her 40's while the producers writing for that viewer are in their 20's. It's not that one is right and one is wrong. But it's a fact that their values and sensibilities are wildly different!

So here it is. This is what you've been waiting for. The real reason you bought this book. I'm about to impart to you, and ONLY you, the secret of life. If you know and understand this simple concept, it will instantly make you a better communicator and change your life forever! Are you ready? The secret is this...

IT'S NOT ABOUT YOU!

That's right! That just happened!! I hope you were sitting down. It's not about what YOU would like to see or hear. It's not about what makes YOU comfortable or think or laugh. It's about what makes your audience comfortable, or think or laugh. Hey, if your happiness coincides with their happiness, that's icing on the cake! Just make sure you're baking that cake for them! Because your audience doesn't really care what suits your taste or how YOU feel. All they really care about is that their needs are being met! When communicators understand the audience, who they are, what they care about and why, it is much easier to craft a presentation specifically designed for them. In turn, the audience has more affinity for the speaker and interest in the subject matter.

SO, WHO IS THIS WOMAN?!?

When I begin working with a news station and I am tasked to elevate a show, I will usually ask the same question to producers and on-camera personnel...

"Who is your target viewer?"

Inevitably I get the same response...

"Whoever is watching!" or, "Everybody!"

Yikes! A 20-year-old has a completely different reality and set of values than a 40-year-old or that of a 60-year-old. People in these different age groups have different goals, sensibilities, lexicons, and daily concerns! So how do you make decisions on the very best way to write a show or stack a show or deliver copy if you have no idea who you're talking to? The answer is, you can't! The more specific you can be with understanding your target viewer, the stronger and more dynamic you will be when crafting a show or performance. Period.

Usually, the easiest and fastest way to find information about your target viewer is to ask the News Director or Sales Department or General Manager. However, to get the ball rolling, here is a basic check-list of subjects that should be researched and data that should be gathered:

Target Viewer: Information Check-List

- ☐ Age
- ☐ Education
- ☐ Occupation
- ☐ Gender

☐ Marital Status

☐ Children

☐ Religion

☐ Political Leaning

☐ Cultural Background

☐ Hobbies / Activities

☐ Interests

Not everyone in the audience will be the same age or have the same amount of education or children. But what you want to find is an average for all these data points so that you come up with a composite target viewer. And then you want to name her. It would look something like this:

Target Viewer
⇒ NAME: Maria
⇒ AGE: 42
⇒ EDUCATION: Junior College - 2 years
⇒ OCCUPATION: Mother, housekeeper, part-time job
⇒ CHILDREN: One pre-teen and one teenager
⇒ MARITAL STATUS: Married
⇒ INTERESTS: Kids, health, cooking, bargains, consumer issues, community safety, etc.

And the list goes on. But you get the idea. Once you have this information it becomes easier to choose how to begin a story or which story begins the show or how to stack a show or which stories we should tease. Once we know who our target viewer is and we have a name for her, we should begin making our choices by asking, "Would this tease compel Maria to watch the story?" "Would Maria want to listen to this story after hearing this lead?" "Would Maria CARE?!?

Of course, there will always be news stories that must be included in your show that Maria wouldn't care about. In these cases, the question becomes, does that story really need to be teased? Does it really need to lead the show or even be in the first block? And because of its significance, you might decide that it does. In this case, you want to do everything in your ability to craft it and deliver it so that Maria finds it interesting.

Chapter 5

CRAFTING YOUR STORY

"Brevity is the soul of wit."
Shakespeare.

Everything you learned in your journalism classes about writing is excellent. Include the who, what, where, when, why and how. Never inject your opinion. Use short sentences. Always begin with the most recent event. Never use the word "I." Avoid jargon, clichés, fad words, and so on. Seriously, all great stuff. I'm not here to blast academic learning because, if it was a good education and you were diligent with your studies (after all, the teacher is only as good as the student), then you have a strong grasp of grammar and structure as well, which tends to be important as a writer.

Once you leave academia and enter the cold cruel world of broadcast news however, you find that these strong basics of writing are just that... basics. Producers and writers who only follow those journalism precepts have the tendency to craft copy that can come across as institutional or staid. The biproduct is a persona, reading that copy, appearing unfeeling, robotic or stiff. What we're about here, is enhancing your academic knowledge with the dynamic elements necessary to be a successful storyteller in today's commercial world of broadcast news. I know, blasphemy, right? Just putting the words 'commercial' and 'news' in the same sentence makes me want to go take a *Silkwood* shower. The only consolation I can offer you is this: the following course of mastery won't rob you of your integrity or your soul. In fact, it will bolster the 'personality' inherent in your persona, making your performance much more compelling and giving you the single strongest tool a communicator can wield... the human condition!

Strong writing ensures that headlines, teases and leads consistently capture the essence of the story. Compelling writing uses the most powerful visual language that is appropriate to the piece. And when a story is beautifully crafted, it is concise, conversational, human condition oriented, viewer centric, compelling, urgent, and just a bit edgy.

ROMANTIC REALITY

Before we jump into the discussion of crafting your story, I want to say a quick word about the general principle of being 'conversational.' It is an industry wide rule that we 'write like people talk.' And on the face of it, this seems like a no-brainer. Stay away from words like perp, tort and malfeasance and you should be fine, right? We don't want to talk to 'Maria' on the air any differently than we would talk to her at the grocery store.

At the same time, we need to keep in mind that TV reality is very different than real-life reality. It's what I like to call, "Romantic Reality." TV gives us the perception of reality, but at the end of the day, nobody really talks that way or looks that way or behaves that way. Certainly not all the time. It's a heightened sense of reality. The next time you watch your favorite TV series, pay close attention to the dialogue. Although the actors make it sound 'conversational,' nobody actually speaks that quickly in complete paragraphs without grammatical errors, regionalisms, or crutch phrases. Unless the actor is playing a character with a peculiar speech pattern or dialect, the copy is mostly uniform, clean, and concise. You won't hear any glitches like 'ums' or 'uhs,' you won't hear characters chat about nothing for a few minutes in a circuitous manner until actually having a point, and you won't hear any colloquialisms like "wanna," "gonna," "ya know," or "I mean."

All this to say, much of the do's and don'ts we're about to discuss have very little to do with the 'normal reality' of our daily lives. But it does feed viewers the way they like to be fed… with Romantic Reality.

THE HIGH CONCEPT

I lived in Los Angeles from 1979 through the mid-90's. During that time, I was an actor, taught at the Beverly Hills Playhouse, directed theatre and wrote when I got the inspiration. As a writer I had my fair share of rejections as well as a few successes. But my biggest lesson came when I tried to get my best friend Buddy, an executive producer at Universal Studios, to read my script.

I caught up to Buddy on the studio lot as he was walking from his office to one of his sets currently in production. Before he knew what was happening, I handed him my script.

"What's this?" Buddy asked.

"It's very good!" I said.

He realized what I handed him, handed it back then walked faster. I picked up my pace to keep up.

"Yeah," he said with a patronizing smile, "I'm not reading that."

"What if it's the next *Star Wars*?!?" I asked.

He suddenly stopped and looked at me intently.

"Is it the next *Star Wars*?" he asked.

"Uh, sure. Add a few light sabers. A spaceship. Set it in the past... or the future. Were they in the past? I never could figure that out."

Exasperated, Buddy continued walking.

"Whatever. Just tell me the high concept." Buddy commanded.

"The what?" I asked.

"Look, I don't care what's in a script. I can have a script rewritten," he said, looking at me like we both knew mine would have to be rewritten. And this was my BEST friend.

"All I care about is, can I sell it," Buddy said. "And for that I need a high concept."

"It's called, '*Pebbles Revenge*'," I said, proudly.

"Sounds like a breakfast cereal that gives children the runs." He said. Then he stopped suddenly and turned to look at me.

"Is it about a breakfast cereal that gives children the runs?" he asked.

"Is it about diarrheic children?" I asked. I couldn't figure out whether he was being hopeful or just messing with me.

"I could write that!" I said. "In the opening credits we would find a prepubescent Montezuma frantically searching for a clean banana leaf."

He thought about that for a New York second then turned away.

"I need to get to my set," he said, waking faster. I chased after.

"Just tell me what you need, and I'll write it!" I begged.

"I need a HIGH concept! A word, phrase or sentence that tells me everything I need to know about the story," he said. "Something dynamic. Something I can SELL!"

"You mean like, *Ghostbusters*, *Dirty Dancing*, *The Terminator*," I said.

"Exactly!" he said. Let me know when you know!"

And with that, he was gone. Along with my dreams for *Pebbles Revenge.*

High concepts are instrumental in promoting books, films, products, and stories. Look at magazine covers. They hook their customers by headlines that go right to the heart of their stories. Four or five words that are all about the human condition without apology or justifiers. Four or five words that compel and energize. Some examples of high concepts:

High Concept Book Titles
- *How to Win Friends and Influence People*
- *The Power of Your Subconscious Mind*
- *How Not to Die - Foods that Prevent Disease*

High Concept Film Titles
- *The Texas Chainsaw Massacre*
- *Twelve Years a Slave*
- *Snakes on a Plane*

High Concept News Teases (recent examples from various local markets)
- A mother helplessly watches in horror as road rage threatens her newborn.
- A crime alert for the gun-toting crooks that beat a business owner and stole his life savings.
- A father abandons his two-year-old daughter so that he can party.
- Catfights ensue over church run daycare.
- A murder suspect representing himself walks out of his own trial.

When you're ready to craft the tease, lead or headline of your story, it's best to think in terms of a high concept. The best high concepts are concise, human condition statements that embody the essence of the story and compel the target audience to listen.

WRITE VISUALLY

The strongest element of communication is visual. In Chapter 2 we discussed the importance of this concept when presenting yourself so that viewers have the perception that you belong in your position, that you are approachable, strong, and that you should be listened to and trusted. In the context of storytelling, the master communicator will utilize words that illicit the strongest visual images in the viewer's mind. Compare these examples:

1) She got to the other side of the field quickly.
2) She ran to the other side of the field.
3) She sprinted to the other side of the field with all her might.

The first sentence gives the viewer a general idea of what happened. But it's difficult to visualize since there are many modes of transportation. We don't know if she was carried over, hauled over or used her own two feet. And if she crossed the field on her own, did she walk, hop, or shuffle quickly? Exasperating, I know. Just think about your poor viewer!

The second example gives a better indication of how to visualize the event, but it's still general. Don't take my word for it. Look up synonyms for "run." Sprint, race, dart, dash, gallop, streak, bolt… you get the idea. The more specific you can be, the better the viewer can visualize, the better you are as a communicator.

The third example is the most powerful. It uses the phrases "sprinted" and "all her might" to draw the strongest images for the viewer to process. I understand that not every news story lends itself to using visual language. But when it does, it is incumbent on the storyteller to do so. And because we tend to write the same kinds of stories over-and-over again, it is easy to fall into the trap of using the same lexicon to tell those stories. Do yourself a favor and use a thesaurus occasionally. It will make you a better craftsman and more interesting to your viewers.

BE CONCISE

Thomas Jefferson said it best, "The most valuable of all talents is that of never using two words when one will do." Using short one-idea sentences is the goal. This seems like such a simple rule but the amount of bloated and superfluous writing in broadcast news is astounding. And it happens in EVERY market. Much of the overwriting comes in the form of redundancy which softens the edge, kills urgency and ultimately weakens the message. Here's an example of a story that was recently aired in a top 20 market. See if you can identify areas of opportunity for edits that would tighten up the piece. (I have changed the names to protect the innocent.)

A HEARTBREAKING ANNIVERSARY TODAY FOR THE FAMILY OF MISSING NURSING STUDENT KATIE SMITH.

MISSING NOW FOR TEN MONTHS TODAY, THIS MORNING PEOPLE IN KATIE'S HOMETOWN ARE MAKING SURE SHE IS NOT FORGOTTEN.

IN FACT, THE STUDENTS AT HOMEDALE HIGH SCHOOL IN FRANKLIN WILL BE TAKING PART IN BRING KATIE HOME DAY. SPECIAL T-SHIRTS AND PINK RIBBONS WILL BE WORN BY THE STUDENTS.

ORGANIZERS ARE HOPING IT WILL ENCOURAGE KATIE'S FAMILY. IT ALL COMES AS A NEW PUSH IS UNDERWAY TO FIND MORE INFORMATION ABOUT THAT NURSING STUDENT WHO'S BEEN MISSING NOW.

THE REWARD FOR HER SAFE RETURN HAS JUMPED ALL THE WAY UP TO 250,000 DOLLARS. THAT HAPPENED EARLIER THIS MONTH.

There is never just one way to write anything, so this isn't about writing the perfect story. It's about understanding some of the tools we have at our disposal to make the writing more concise so that it is a BETTER story.

➤ **Subjective Adjectives.** Be careful of using words like, "Bizarre," "Fantastic," "Astonishing," "Breathtaking" and "Unbelievable." It is true that they are all human condition in nature. But often, your story won't stand up to this kind of hyperbole and it will weaken the piece. In this case, leading with "HEARTBREAKING" is overdramatizing and, as we find later in the piece, untrue. The day is supposed to be one of encouragement, not mourning.

➤ **Misused/Incorrect Terms.** "ANNIVERSARY" is misused here since anniversaries are measured in years, not months. I guess we could call this 'dramatic license,' but for what purpose? It does nothing to further the story and the falsehood only weakens the message.

➤ **Begin with a High Concept**. Look at the lead again. It is one of despair when the story is one of hope. It suggests the story is about the family instead of the hometown and high school students. And it is passive; promises us nothing and takes us nowhere. In fact, the line in this story that is closer to a high concept is in the third graph, "THE STUDENTS AT HOMEDALE HIGH SCHOOL IN FRANKLIN WILL BE TAKING PART IN BRING KATIE HOME DAY."

➤ **Eradicate Redundancies**. Repetition soften the edge and kills urgency. The concept of 'today' is echoed five times with the words, "TODAY," "NOW," "THIS MORNING," "DAY," and "NOW" again. The word "MISSING" is stated three times and the phrase "NURSING STUDENT" is stated twice.

➤ **Eradicate Helping Verbs**. Helping verbs are forms of the verbs, "be," "do," "have," and "will," when followed by another verb in order to form a question, a negative sentence, a compound tense, or the passive. Helping verbs are no help to you and only weaken the message. Some of the phrases with helping verbs in this story are:

 o "ARE MAKING SURE," should be, "MAKE SURE."

 o "WILL BE TAKING PART," should be, "WILL TAKE PART."

 o "ARE HOPING IT WILL," should be, "HOPE TO."

➤ **Eradicate Superfluous Information**. In the end this story tells us that the reward has jumped, but never tells us where it began. It could have just ended with the reward amount for her safe return and completely cut the last sentence, "THAT HAPPENED EARLIER THIS MONTH."

➤ **Write in the Active Voice**. Passive voice uses verb phrases with a form of the verb "to be." The receiver of the action usually precedes the verb: *The boy was bitten.*

In passive voice writing, the actor often appears in a prepositional phrase: *The boy was bitten by the hungry lion.*

Sentences in passive voice lack immediacy and require the viewer to jump back and forth for meaning. In active voice writing, the receiver of the verb's action follows the verb: *The hungry lion bit the man.*

Always use the active voice and present tense when possible because it is more concise and adds a sense of immediacy which is both more compelling and urgent. In the case of this story...

Passive Voice:
SPECIAL T-SHIRTS AND PINK RIBBONS WILL BE WORN BY THE STUDENTS.

Active Voice:
THE STUDENTS WILL WEAR SPECIAL T-SHIRTS AND PINK RIBBONS.

HUMAN CONDITION VERSUS INSTITUTIONAL COPY

Always begin with the human condition. Period. I don't think I can be any clearer than that. It is the first rule in great storytelling. Headlines, teases and leads should have the human condition at their beginning and at their core.

The opposite of human condition writing is what's commonly known as institutional writing. Institutional writing begins headlines, teases and leads with names, numbers, titles, or organizations. This is a problem because, for the most part; names, numbers, titles and organizations have no one human condition attached to them. Begin a story with, "Tarrant County Police are searching for a suspect," and no one will care because there is no one human condition attached to 'Tarrant County Police.' Couple that with the fact this lead says nothing more than the police are doing their jobs, make for a message that is stagnant and uninteresting. Begin that same story by saying, "A baby-killer is on the run in Tarrant County," and heads will turn.

I am not suggesting that you should be 'sensational' with your copy. What I am suggesting is that many times the human condition will be buried in a story when it should be front and center. And if your argument for starting in an institutional fashion and burying that human condition is that you didn't want to give away your 'best' stuff up front, there's a good chance you'll lose the viewer before they ever get to hear your 'best stuff!' If you begin with the human condition, they will want to hear the data. If you begin with data, no one will care.

A WORD ABOUT BEGINNING WITH THE WORD, "POLICE"

DON'T!

The only time you should begin your headline, tease or lead with the word "Police" or "Investigators" is when the story is

ABOUT the police or investigators. Beginning with "Police" is about as institutional as it gets. And, quite frankly, since most stories come from the police, to begin in that fashion is just lazy writing. And while we're at it, please avoid using the old and tired cliché, "Police are asking for your help," unless it's necessary and true.

WRITE WITH AN 'EDGE'

When I suggest writing should have an edge, the first thing most folks think I'm asking them to be is confrontational. And although there could certainly be an element of that in the work, writing with an edge means crafting a message that is daring or provocative or intense or exciting. It's exactly the opposite of what I call, "soft copy."

WRITING with EDGE	SOFT COPY
Pointed, Daring, Clear, Provocative, Intense, Exciting	Indecisive, Nebulous, Boring, Unexciting, Stagnant, Institutional

To illustrate what I mean by 'soft copy,' let's look at the beginning line from a story I came across while coaching another client station a few years back. Take a minute to review this lead and see how many words or phrases you can pick out that are considered soft.

TEXAS STATE OFFICIALS SAY THAT A STUDY SHOWS HOW SOME FRATERNITY PRACTICES COULD BE CAUSING THEIR FRAT MEMBERS TO PERFORM POORLY ON THEIR EXAMS.

✓ **"TEXAS STATE" is soft**. Locators are considered soft because they alienate viewers who do not live in that location. Remember that viewers watch the local news for very selfish reasons. If the first thing they hear is that the story is about a man living in another town or in another state, their tendency will be to instantly disengage since they believe the story won't affect them. Locators must be included in the story, to be sure, but they are not necessary in the lead and certainly not at the very beginning of the piece.

There is a caveat to this. If the locator is vital to the core of the story or tied to the human condition of the story, then it should be front and center. Locators like, "Twin Towers," "Ground Zero," "Columbine" and "Sandy Hook" are all instantly associated with very specific human conditions and would easily draw attention at the beginning of a piece.

✓ **"OFFICIALS" is soft**. Officials are no different than police or investigators. They are all considered 'institutional' and therefore soft. It is vitally important to have them in the body of the story. But unless the story is about the officials, keep them out of the lead line.

✓ **"SAY" is soft**. Attributions are soft unless being said by someone with a high degree of human condition attached to his/her persona. But that would be rare since broadcast news is the organization that has vilified everybody. Yesterday we presented a story that lawyers lie more than half the time, but today we're telling you to listen to this other story because, "Lawyers say…" As with most of these examples, it is vitally important that we have attributions in the body of our story, just do your best to keep them out of the lead.

✓ **"A STUDY SHOWS" is soft**. Empirical data is soft. Last year we told you that a study shows coffee is bad for you. This year we're citing another study that says it will make you live forever! The fact is that most of these studies aren't even scientific theory. (A body of facts must be repeatedly confirmed through observation and experiment to become scientific theory.) Because of this, viewers don't really hold, "A study shows," as all that significant. Other empirical data statements to avoid in your leads are, "A poll states," "A new report released today," and "New numbers show." Should they be in your story? YES! Should they be in your headline, tease or lead? NO!

✓ **"SOME" and "COULD" are soft**. Conditional words such as 'some,' 'may,' 'might,' 'should,' 'could,' 'usually,' 'possibly,' and 'probably,' are ambiguous and therefore considered 'soft,' Guard against using conditional language, especially in headlines teases and leads as it weakens the message.

On a side note, I see much more conditional language woven into the copy of Southern markets than I do Northern markets. I believe it's because the Southern lexicon is very conditional. For instance:

A Southerner will say:

> "You might wanna to try that tea. It is possibly the best tea you will ever have."

A Northerner will say:

> "Drink the tea! It's good. We gotta go!"

I always tell my clients that we're working towards having a Northern lexicon with a Southern charm.

✓   **"BE" is soft**. Auxiliary Verbs or Helping Verbs are forms of the verbs 'be,' 'do,' 'have,' and 'will' when they are followed by another verb in order to form a question, a negative sentence, a compound tense or the passive. Auxiliary verbs weaken the message, are considered "soft" and should be avoided when writing headlines, teases and leads. Examples:

1) "PRACTICES COULD BE CAUSING THEIR FRAT MEMBERS..." The conditional word "COULD" and the auxiliary verb "BE" weakens this phrase. Cut those out and a stronger phrase emerges:

    PRACTICES CAUSE THEIR FRAT MEMBERS

2) "THERE WERE REPORTS THAT HE WAS CHOOSING NOT TO GO." The auxiliary verb here is "WAS." Cut that out for the stronger phrase:

    "THERE WERE REPORTS THAT HE CHOSE NOT TO GO."

3) "A CITY INSPECTOR IS FACING NEW CHARGES TONIGHT." Cut out the auxiliary verb "IS" to read:

    "A CITY INSPECTOR FACES NEW CHARGES TONIGHT."

✓   **"FRAT" is soft**. We already used FRATERNITY earlier in this sentence so FRAT becomes redundant. Redundancy softens the edge and kills urgency.

So what's left? After taking out all the 'soft' copy? We've gone from this…

TEXAS STATE OFFICIALS SAY THAT A STUDY SHOWS HOW SOME FRATERNITY PRACTICES COULD BE CAUSING THEIR FRAT MEMBERS TO PERFORM POORLY ON THEIR EXAMS.

To this…

FRATERNITY PRACTICES CAUSE MEMBERS TO PERFORM POORLY ON THEIR EXAMS.

We can now tweak what remains in this lead to be more compelling (one possibility would be changing the word "practices" to "traditions"), but at least now that we have taken out all the soft language, we have a concise and certainly stronger lead that compels us to listen. The body of the story can then lay out the attributions and officials and studies and which members are affected.

ODDS AND ENDS

There are a few more common mistakes I see in most news shops around the country.

➢ **Avoid beginning sentences with "There is" or "There are."** This isn't a big one but I see it enough to make mention here. "There are many people who drink," should be, "Many people drink."

➢ **"Local" is usually superfluous which makes it soft.** If you're at a 'local' station and it's the 'local news' then there's no need to begin by saying, "A local man, today." If I'm watching the 'local news' then I assume everything I see is about local stuff unless you tell me otherwise. The time to use the word 'local' is as a comparison to make the fact stand out. "Nationally, everyone is doing so-and-so, but a local man today…"

➢ **Avoid using filler adjectives and adverbs!** Very rarely if ever should these words be used. They are superfluous and many times weaken the meaning or energy of the message.

- o **"Obviously."** If it's so obvious, why are you wasting my time talking about it?

- o **"Basically" or "Essentially."** Using these words brings up more question than it answers. "The law basically says…" begs the question, what does the law REALLY say? Using these terms also makes it seem that you're not sure about the intricacies of the subject matter.

- o **"Literally."** I heard this on-air just the other day and had to laugh; "It was literally raining cats and dogs!" No, it wasn't. Seriously, it wasn't!

- o **"Again" or "As I said" or "As we told you earlier,"** **etc.** When the mind hears these kinds of phrases, it will disengage or become annoyed because redundancy is worthless and annoying. It is true; part of your job in the news business is to repeat yourself. Just don't tell the viewer that you're doing it. And find a different way of saying it the second (or third) time around.

➢ **Avoid using hyperbolic adjectives.** If you use a word like 'bizarre,' 'fantastic,' 'astonishing,' 'breathtaking' or 'unbelievable,' then what your describing had better be exactly that. If it isn't, you're just hurting your credibility with the viewer. Remember, your viewers have been watching TV for 20-40 years and have already heard and seen just about everything. So there isn't much you can tell them that's "bizarre" or "unbelievable."

TEASING TIPS

Everything we've discussed about crafting your story applies to teasing as well. Here are a few more tips to keep in mind.

➢ **Consider writing your tease like you would a movie trailer.** Strong movie trailers are not coy or ambiguous. They show highlights of the film and promise the viewer more of the same. The tease is not about getting the viewer to like you. The tease is about impinging the viewer with an emotional absolute imperative to see your story.

➢ **Promise more than what the viewer already expects**. "Your weathercaster will be back with your forecast," or "We'll explain what they say happened," isn't much of a tease.

➢ **Keep your promise**! Too often I see this kind of exchange between Anchor and Reporter:

> ANCHOR: Today Chief Smith spoke with (reporter) about a strategy to stop the violence. (Reporter) now joins us live. (Reporter), what kind of plan is he talking about?

> REPORTER: The chief didn't give us exact details, but he said it will take a group effort.

If the viewers can't trust that you'll deliver on your promise, they will have no use for you.

➤ **Don't promise an interview.** Instead, pick the best part of the interview and promise that aspect. If the interview hasn't happened, promise to ask a compelling question or promise to hit on a hot-button topic.

➤ **Hyperbole makes you sound like a used car salesman.**
"THIS NEXT STORY SOUNDS LIKE SOMETHING OUT OF A MOVIE! BUT IT'S ALMOST TOO BIZARRE TO BELIEVE... BUT YOU KNOW WHAT THEY SAY... TRUTH CERTAINLY IS STRANGER THAN FICTION!"
Stop it. Just, stop it.

➤ **Questions are soft.** Instead of asking, "How can you improve your sex life?" state, "How you can improve your sex life!"

➤ **"If You" statements are soft.** "If you shop at the mall, you'll love this next story," alienates viewers who don't shop at that mall.

➤ **The Double Hook.** Most teases are at least two beats long, but the second beat is usually superfluous.

"A TWENTY-FOUR-CAR PILE-UP ON THE FREEWAY! WE'LL SHOW IT TO YOU WHEN WE RETURN."

One way of making teases more compelling is to make sure that BOTH beats hook the viewer.

"A TWENTY-FOUR-CAR PILE-UP ON THE FREEWAY, AND ALL CAUSED BY A PUPPY OFF OF HIS LEASH!"

Double-hook teases are much more compelling and energizing.

Chapter 6

TELLING YOUR STORY

The devil isn't in the details unless you put him there.
The actual quote is, "God is in the details."

It always baffles me when parents ask how long it will take and how much I would charge to give their children talent. Yep, that's what they ask me to provide. Talent! Of course, then I became a parent. You learn very quickly as a parent that you will do just about anything for your kids. Even ask the impossible. And asking for talent is asking for the impossible. Because talent is a God-given thing. You can't buy talent or gain it through positive thinking or build it through hard work. The truth of it is, you're either born with an aptitude for doing a thing, or you're not. Some folks are born with a lot, some with a little, and some with none at all.

Now, technique is another matter altogether. You're not born with technique. Technique is something you can gain along the way through coaching and training or trial-and-error or just living your life. The more technique you have, the more it will support your natural abilities and allow them to shine, unimpeded. Consider your favorite stand-up comedians. Their seemingly effortless ability to command an audience for one hour took hundreds of hours doing the same kinds of jokes for countless audiences to perfect a rhythm and timing. Were they already born with the talent for comedy? Certainly. But talent doesn't guarantee success. Gaining technique through practice is what turns good into great. Show me a professional with a consistent long-lasting successful career, and I'll show you someone with an abundance of hard-earned technique that gives them the ability to produce consistent quality.

A talented storyteller with a great skill-set can take a mediocre script and make it sound better. A great script can't do anything for a lousy storyteller. I love Shakespeare. When it's performed well, there's nothing better. Unfortunately, I've had to suffer through a lot of community theatre and showcases over the years, watching bad actors desecrate the Bard. There's nothing more painful. Shakespeare cannot make bad actors better. It's like the old joke about the farmer attempting to teach a pig how to sing. In the end, the only thing it produces is a frustrated farmer. And it annoys the hell out of the pig.

The bottom line? I can't give you (or your kids) talent. But what I can do is offer you techniques that develop talented on-camera personalities into great storytellers.

WATCHING VERSUS LISTENING

You can't assume that your viewer is just sitting on the coach riveted by your presentation, eyes glued to your every move. We know for a fact that at any point during a newscast, most viewers are not watching, but listening while they perform other tasks. Therefore, how you tell your story is just as important as the visuals. Great storytelling demands the ability to deliver in such a way that the viewer can picture and feel what the communicator is saying without ever having to look at the screen. This requires the communicator to highlight the human conditions within the story by utilizing emotional tones, transitions, phrasing, and all the other storytelling techniques inherent in conversational speech.

I've heard many justifications over the years as to why on-camera personalities aren't using as much vocal variety as they could. The three most common excuses are these:

1) **"I don't want to seem biased!"** I hear this one a lot. It usually harkens back to their university journalism indoctrination requiring objectivity in reporting, delivering in a neutral and unbiased manner. And I totally agree that the viewer shouldn't know what side of the issue the reporter or anchor embraces when communicating a 'hard news' story, especially if it's about politics or religion or sexual orientation. But what if the story is about killing children or preventing pedophilia or curing cancer? If you delivered those stories in a monotone fashion, the viewer would be more distracted (and disturbed) by your indifference than be interested in the piece.

Another thing to consider here is that tone of voice helps the viewer to process the information correctly. The phrase, "It's going to snow!" presented in a monotone delivery means very little. Those same words delivered with a smile suggests playtime. Delivered with a harsh tone, the viewers are warned to prepare for a rough event.

2) **"I don't want to come across as clownish."** Clients will say they've seen attempts by others to emote look stupid and don't want to fall into the same trap. So here's the thing… just because you see someone drive a car into a wall doesn't mean driving is bad. It only means that driver didn't know how to drive a car. The fact is, you're being paid to make a message come alive on camera with as

much energy and humanity as is possible and appropriate to the piece.

Viewers best remember facts when they are attached to emotional impact. If a story is written in a balanced fashion and you are true to the words, you can tell the story with feeling and still be objective and a lot more effective and memorable.

3) **"We've done this story a thousand times."** I hear this a lot from morning folks who are doing three and four hours straight, every morning. So, I figure you only have three choices: 1) Kill the story. 2) Run a crawl during your read that says, "I know you're tired of listening to it, I'M tired of SAYING it! But if you'll just hang on, the show gets REALLY good in the third block." or 3) Deliver the story as if it were the first time! Because that is, after all, why you get paid the big bucks. It's your job to make it sound as if it were the first time, every time. Of course, it wouldn't hurt if it could be written a bit differently for each half-hour. I'm just sayin'...

UTILIZE THE HUMAN CONDITION

➤ **Disney World**. Telling the kids, you'll be taking them for a 17-hour drive, and assuming they'll go peacefully and quietly as you stuff them into the car, would be insanity. On the other hand, telling them up front that you're going to Disney World would be enough to get them into the back seat and quiet, even before asking if they'd like to take the ride. Beginning your story with institutional copy is like asking your viewers to get in a car for a 17-hour ride. They won't want to go. On the other hand, if you give them the human condition up front, in the tease, headline and lead, they will be much more willing to take the ride.

> **Reengage the ear!** Here's what we know...

1) Viewers are mostly listening instead of watching.

2) To keep viewers listening, their attention must be reengaged every 10 seconds by triggering a picture or emotion in their mind.

3) Human condition words and phrases elicit pictures and emotions in the mind.

> **Pop those human condition words:** Be aware of the words you deliver that have the human condition. Attach appropriate emotional tones to those words to make them sound like what they mean.

PREPARATION

At the risk of sounding like a nagging parent, proper preparation is a key to long-term success. It produces consistency and a higher-quality of work. Since your job is to communicate, what do you do each day and before every show to prepare as a communicator? Not as a writer. Not as an editor. Not as a producer. As a COMMUNICATOR?

> **Preparing Copy.** Tone of voice (emotional tones) is the single strongest vocal communicator. Take note of the emotional tones and colorations in teases, headlines and stories. Break them down to the essential human condition words and phrases most important to those interested viewers, and then decide what emotional tones you will attach to those human condition words and phrases. This will help you

achieve vocal variety within the stories and clarify the transitions between stories.

➢ **Pre-Show Prompter Warm-up**. Get out there a few minutes before the show and warm-up with the prompter. Read at least one story with your full voice and with a full delivery of emotions. This will work out any glitches and allow you to springboard into the show.

➢ **Review Airchecks**. To speed up the development of your skills, it is important to monitor yourself on a regular basis. For objectivity; to see and hear your presentation way viewers do, review each aircheck twice; once without picture and once without sound.

  ✓ **Watch without audio**. Are you in perpetual motion? Do you turn profile or turn your back to the audience? Are you where you need to be when you need to be there? Look for all the elements in Chapter Two during this aircheck review.

  ✓ **Listen without watching**. Are you talking too fast or too slow? Are you talking to your viewer or at her? Are you making clear transitions when necessary? Are you using crutch phrases? Are you weaving the human condition throughout your presentation? Are you being conditional or being redundant?

CONVERSATIONAL ELEMENTS

Once the story is written and you have identified all the words and phrases with the human condition. It is time to take off the writer's hat and put on the communicator's hat. Deciding how to deliver the copy and rehearsing those decisions are vital for the master communicator.

➤ **Emotional tone.** The emotional quality of the voice -- loving, harsh, compassionate, sarcastic -- that sets the mood of a word, phrase or story. Communication without emotional tone is flat and uninteresting. More to the point, it isn't human. In fact, it is almost impossible to communicate without the auditor comprehending an attached tone. Even if tone is unintended by the communicator.

That is the interesting thing about human beings. They are not satisfied with nothingness. They will not accept a void. Presented with empty space, they will fill it with something. When a communicator realizes that the audience will assign emotional tones where none exists and that the choice of emotional tones is just as important as the choice of words, the ability to choose and deliver the appropriate emotional tones becomes a real asset.

➤ **Punching Versus Tone.** Punching words may give delivery a limited amount of vocal variety, but it makes the speaker sound officious and detached. It is often overused in broadcast news. People don't punch words in day-to-day conversation. Instead, they attach emotional tones to the words and phrases that have the human condition. Tone (coloring words with emotion) is the strongest tool you have as a communicator. Communicating to highlight the human condition through coloring words with emotional tones can mark the difference between sounding conversational and sounding pedantic.

➤ **Avoid emphasizing insignificant words at the expense of more important words around them.** "She was charged with injury TO a child." What was she charged with?

"INJURY to a CHILD." Look for the "who, what, when, where, why" when making inflection choices.

➤ **Voice color:** Tone's baby brother is voice color; making words sound like what they mean in that context. For example, saying "fast" quickly, "slow" drawn out, "explosion" with a pop, and "sleepy" in a soft and soothing voice are all instances of using voice color.

➤ **Duration.** How long a word -- usually a vowel sound -- is held. "Two years" delivered holding the vowels (long duration) sounds longer.

➤ **Energy!** Energy is not 'louder' or 'faster.' These conditions are possible if you have energy, but they don't necessarily create energy. The potential to increase the energy of your presentation depends on your commitment to the message, and communicating the message with a high investment in the human conditions inherent in that message. High energy is also characterized by a conversational quality. And remember to keep your energy consistent throughout the newscast. It shouldn't drop from interaction to news or from hard news to soft.

➤ **Pitch.** How high or low the voice is on the "musical scale." Especially effective when reading sentences with parenthetical thoughts.

➤ **Inflection.** Changing pitch within a single word. In phrasing, inflection helps to connect a key word to the rest of its modifiers; one-word stress will chop it off from its modifiers.

➢ **The Pause.** Don't think of it as 'dead-air.' It is a purposeful stoppage of sound to attract attention or give emphasis. This is different than hesitation, which usually results in an "uh" verbalizing the pause.

➢ **Pace versus Rate**. Rate is the speed of delivery; how fast the communicator reads or speaks. Pace is the ebb and flow of storytelling; including pauses, intense passages and the full range of dramatic relief. Most communicators lose their pace when they push their reading or speaking speed past their natural limits. They also lose meaning, intensity, interpretation and emotional range. They swallow words, they skip periods. Use effective pauses, phrasing and vary the tone of your stories.

➢ **Contrasting tones:** A well written story will have contrasts to highlight differences between ideas or further an understanding of the same idea.

> THE COACH'S DECISION ANGERED THE PARENTS WHICH MADE THE KIDS EVEN HAPPIER!

The added contrasting tone 'happier' gives the coach's decision so much more weight than if we had only mentioned the parents' reaction.

Endeavor to find and express contrasting tones in every story. This will give the copy more texture and help to highlight the major tonal elements.

➢ **Build lists.** The statement "robbed, raped, and then murdered" is different than the phrase "robbed, murdered and then raped." The distinction should be evident, not only in the writing, but in the vocal build and tonal emphasis placed on each word. Whether your list is a group of words or a succession of sentences, they need to be delivered with a gradient or with variety.

➤ **He said, she said.** A good storyteller will relate the ideas or words of a person by communicating them with a shade of the same style or tone or intention that was used by that person. Since the viewer wasn't there, it is the job of the storyteller to relate the story in such a way that the viewer can see it, smell it, taste it, touch it, and feel it.

➤ **The soft comma.** Ours is a language of phrases, not sentences. It is a tendency when delivering copy to read the entire sentence from start to finish without a beat. However, people rarely do this in normal conversation. When prepping your copy, look for opportunities to phrase things by placing 'soft commas' in your sentences. A 'soft comma' is a place in the sentence where you have decided to add a quick beat or pause.

➤ **Transitions.** Transitions are the road signs that keep the viewer with you. You need to add change of tone, pitch, or some other technique to emphasize them for the viewer.

➤ **Use periods.** There must be vocal punctuation to separate thoughts and ideas. Without this, nothing takes on any importance and everything runs together. Avoid blasting through the ends of sentences.

SING-SONG

Sing-song is a term referring to a person's voice as having a monotonous cadence or a repeated rising and falling rhythm.

Sing-song is something we want to avoid as it gets annoying. Really, really annoying.

➢ **Monitor yourself for falling into the habit of ending sentences with the same downward inflection.** Many newscasters, seemingly in an effort to sound more 'newsy,' will end every hard-news story with the same tone. Occasionally ending with a downward inflection can be effective. Doing it all the time sounds robotic and stiff.

➢ **Don't let recurring sentence structures dictate your rhythm.** Different writers have different writing styles, but each writer tends to stick with the same sentence structure throughout his/her style. If you don't pay attention, repetitive sentence structures can force you into making each sentence sound the same, even though they have different messages and contain different human condition elements. Watch out for pattern emphasis of any sort that seems to be replacing conversational delivery. If you feel lost or as if you have no perspective on how you're doing, just focus on the meaning of the words you're saying.

➢ **Don't trail off at the ends of your sentences.** This happens mostly when the last sentence of the story is a throwaway line like, "That investigation continues." or "We're still gathering more information." Dropping energy and volume will disengage the viewer's ear. End as strong as you begin!

➢ **Avoid a pattern that attaches to habit rather than meaning.** Maintain an awareness of news interpretation as conversation. Meaningful conversation contains no repetitive patterns. All rhythm, inflection and emphasis are chosen based on their potential for enhancing the meaning of your message and not based on any other criteria.

IF ALL MEN WERE RICH...

Mark Twain wrote, "If all men were rich, all men would be poor!" Following that logic, if everything was red then there would be no color. If everything was beautiful, there would be no beauty. And if every story sounded the same, then it would all sound like nothing. Most of what we've been discussing is to ensure that it all doesn't sound the same. Every story should have its own character. Every sentence its own life.

➤ **Guard against blanketing a whole piece with one tone**. Don't confuse credibility with significance. The story is already significant. There's no need to make your story 'sound' significant by using one stern vocal tone for the whole piece.

➤ **Lowering your voice doesn't give you credibility**. Many people begin in this business by lowering their voices a few octaves to appear more credible. Unfortunately, this baritone blanket also tends to cover up vocal variety and personality.

➤ **Tell instead of read.** As you read a story, don't think of it as reading, think of it as telling the story. After all, who wants to listen to someone read? Keeping in mind the conversational aspects of relating the story will help it seem more immediate, and the importance of the story will be easier to understand.

➤ **Brevity is the soul of wit.** Write shorter to read longer. If the words take every second just to be uttered at their fastest, you leave yourself no time to color the words with greater meaning. If you have a minute, write for 50 seconds, and then take a minute to say it. Less is definitely more.

➤ **Build on your co-anchor's delivery.** Listen to the way your co-anchor delivers the headline or split-lead. Make sure your delivery takes a step up or sounds different in style or rhythm. This will create more consistency with not only a conversational style but one that moves the show forward and is dynamic.

➢ **Avoid telegraphing where you're going.** If the story and the words begin on a happy note then gradually move to sadness or tragedy, the emotional tones used to convey those words should do the same. Avoid beginning with an emotional tone that mirrors the end instead of supporting the beginning.

➢ **Emotional impact.** Viewers are more likely to remember ideas when they are attached to an emotional impact. If your story is well written but done in a flat, uninvolved fashion, the viewer will not find it as effective or compelling.

➢ **Pop at the top!** Headlines, tops of the halves, tops of every story! Springboard into each one as if you were extremely invested in bringing that message to your viewer. Because that's what she wants from you and what she needs to stay engaged.

➢ **Headlines should vary in style and color**. It is true that they need to have energy and urgency. But they also need to communicate the human conditions inherent in the stories that made them headlines to begin with. If you have three different headlines it means you have three completely different stories; which means each read needs to have its own emotional tone, rhythm and style.

➢ **Audio Video Linkage with Headlines.** Ask the producers to red flag headlines attached to compelling video when you are not going to have the opportunity to see that video before the show. To attach the appropriate emotional tones to your delivery you MUST know what you are reading over. Right?

➢ **Invest in those Headlines.** Headlines are your first entrée to the viewers and give them the kind of energy you want them to have for the next 20-30 minutes. Don't throw them away. Prep that copy by choosing the words and phrases with the strongest human conditions and make sure you deliver them with the appropriate emotional tones.

Chapter 7

VOICE AND SPEECH

*Technique frees the spirit so that
talent can dance without impediment.*

Chances are, you underestimate the potential of your own voice and have accepted whatever vocal quality comes to you naturally. If that's the case, you have ignored (or fail to understand) that your voice has the power to completely change the perception viewers have of your character and your personality.

Consider Mike Tyson and Susan Boyle. The visual image projected by these two personalities could not be more diametrically opposed to their own voices and to each other. Mike Tyson looks like a formidable killing machine. But his lisp and high voice make it difficult to take him seriously outside of the ring. Susan Boyle looks like someone's unassuming sweet aunt. But the power of her singing voice commands an awe and respect few singers will ever match.

You probably don't sound like Mike Tyson and you will most likely NEVER sing like Susan Boyle. But proper modulation can bolster your credibility. Well placed resonance can garner you respect. And the quality of your voice can make or break the viewer's perception of who you are and what you are communicating. And those are the facts, mam. Pure and simple.

RESONANCE

The type of sound your voice produces when it reverberates from different areas of your head and chest is its resonance. And one of the biggest areas of opportunity for most broadcasters is understanding how to place and control the voice for optimum resonance. Think of hitting a drum. If it's a large drum with a big surface area, the sound will be deep and full. If it's a tiny drum with a small surface area, the sound will be thin and 'tinny.' Your vocal resonance is no different. When the voice is placed for 'chest resonance,' it will be richer and deeper in tone. When the voice is placed so that it resonates from the muzzle, (generally a combination of the palate and nasal cavities), then the sound will be higher and 'brighter.'

Ideally, the communicator utilizes a balance of chest and muzzle resonance so that the voice has a power and warmth, highlighted with bright and edgy tones. Unfortunately, most broadcasters have never had vocal training so they give very little thought to, or have very little control over where the voice is placed or how to use it. Instead, environment, situations and energy are more likely to play key factors in dictating the placement and quality of their voices. For instance, many live-shot reporters will project loudly at the camera as if it were a viewer standing several feet away, never considering that the viewer's 'ear' (the handheld or lavalier microphone) is only inches away. This extra effort pushes the voice completely into the muzzle and sounds like yelling 'at' the viewer instead of talking 'to' the viewer. This type of resonance can also be caused by being overly excited or speaking faster than normal. Resonating completely from the muzzle is problematic because the sound produced is usually high and harsh, losing vocal variety in the process. It can also make the voice sound young and inexperienced.

The ability to control, properly place and resonate the voice while maintaining a wide range of vocal variety doesn't come naturally to most people. It usually takes vocal training that also promotes breath support and breath control. The next time you review an aircheck, take notice of your vocal quality and placement. If you believe there's room for improvement, my suggestion would be to find a voice (singing) coach that will give you the exercises necessary to strengthen your diaphragm, widen your range and give you a more powerful resonance in your head and chest. Record the lesson and do it on your own a few times each week. After three or four weeks, go back for another lesson. Training your voice is no different than training your muscles at the gym. You don't go to the gym once and expect your body to magically change. It takes a series of visits over months to see a noticeable difference. Same with the voice. If a voice coach is cost prohibitive, try finding a voice major at your local college or university. Most of these students have been doing these kinds of vocal exercises for years and probably wouldn't mind making a few bucks by passing on that knowledge to you. If you take this course of action, in six months or so, you will see a definite improvement in your voice and a heightened sense of confidence in your performance. A couple things to consider:

➢ **Breathiness results from too much breath, too little resonance**. It's weaker than a vocal approach that uses more voice, less breath. An exercise to improve breathiness is to put your thumb and forefinger on either side of your throat. The more breath you use to produce vocal sounds, the less vibration you'll feel. The more resonance you use, the more vibration you'll feel with your fingers.

> **Throat maintenance.** There are a variety of ways to keep your throat clear during a show, especially if you are suffering from a cold or allergies. One remedy that has worked for many of my clients is keeping a thermos of hot tea with lemon and honey on set. Sipping on that during breaks will sooth, keep your mouth from going dry, and open the throat for a stronger resonance.

> **Vocal warm-up exercises.** Relaxing the muscles and articulators before a show makes for a strong springboard into a performance by enhancing vocal quality, articulation and confidence. It also helps to reduce vocal damage. There are a bazillion vocal warm-up exercises you can find on the web or YouTube.

SPEECH

We're told that being 'conversational' is a high-priority goal in broadcast news. The problem is that Georgia conversational is totally different than Boston conversational which is totally different than California Valley conversational. It's not that one is right and one is wrong. People just speak differently depending on what region of the country they are from, the type of education they've been exposed to, the types of people they associate with, their upbringing, and their unique characteristics.

And at the risk of profiling, (something we ALL inadvertently do, to some degree), the moment viewers hear an accent different from their own, they will make an immediate judgement about that person's character or personality. In focus groups, I have heard viewers say that Northerners are temperamental and uninhibited, Southerners are conservative and traditional, and Westerners are liberal about, well, everything... from politics to religion to lifestyle. It doesn't matter that none of these are unequivocally true. It only matters that biases exists and that you understand what you're facing if you have a specific dialect that places your origin in one of these regions.

If you are working in a small market like Johnson City, Tennessee and you happen to have an Eastern Tennessee accent, it won't matter all that much to the station, because most of the folks watching have the same dialect or they are quite used to hearing it all around them in their daily lives. But as you move up in market size, let's say Nashville, Tennessee for instance… even though it's considered 'the South,' hundreds of thousands living there come from all over the country and would find an Eastern Tennessee accent distracting coming from a news anchor. Stations in larger cities want to appeal to everyone in the market, so they tend to hire talent based on an ability to appeal to the masses. And of all the dialects in this country, there is only one that is accepted by just about everyone as being neutral or 'normal,' meaning viewers aren't distracted by the accent when they hear it. It's called Standard American English (SAE).

Taught in our schools and used in most professional communications, SAE is both grammar and language that lacks any distinctly regional, ethnic, or socioeconomic characteristics. It is the main language used by just about everyone on television, which is why it isn't distracting to the viewer, no matter what dialect he or she is personally accustomed to hearing or speaking. As a professional broadcast news talent, if you aspire to move up in market size, it behooves you to make SAE your on-air persona's natural tongue. If you want to eradicate regionalisms in your speech, you can employ a speech coach to give you the necessary correct pronunciations and exercises, or simply go online and find an SAE dialect program. There are even specific programs like, 'Boston to SAE' or 'Southern to SAE.'

Following are the most common SAE deviations I've observed with broadcast news clients and suggestions I've made to them over the years.

> **"For"** is pronounced like "4" (four or fore) instead of "fur" or "fir."

> **"Your"** is pronounced like "4" with a 'y' (or yore) instead of "yer."

> **"Sure"** is pronounced like "shore" instead of "sher."

> **"Just"** is pronounced by adding a "j" to "ust" instead of "jist."

> **"Going"** Don't drop the 'g.' It's go**ing**, not "goin" or "gonna."

> **Don't flip 'd' and 't' sounds** at the ends of words. This is a very common regionalism in many Southern dialects.

> **Don't neglect the 'g' sound in words that end in "gth."** This is common in Northeastern regions. It's "strength," not "strenth." It's "length," not "lenth."

> **"Often."** In SAE the word "often" has no "t" sound. It should be pronounced like, "soften" without the 's.'

> **"Especially."** The correct pronunciation of this word has no "k" sound.

> **Doesn't vs. Don't.** Remember that "Doesn't" refers to the singular and "don't" refers to the plural. HE doesn't. THEY don't.

➢ **Eradication exercises.** Work on eradicating the "um" and "uh" phrasing in your speech (as well as colloquialisms like "gonna" or "I mean") by challenging yourself during phone conversations not to utter them. Once you've mastered that challenge, take it to your daily interpersonal communications. As you master these challenges, the positive results will also show up in your on-air delivery by osmoses.

➢ **Articulation exercise.** Create a five-sentence paragraph or poem using as many words possible that have the sound you find most difficult. Practice it five times a day for five weeks. If you are still having trouble with articulating that sound, create a new paragraph and continue the process. The proper articulation will eventually find its way into your normal speech pattern. Here's an example for words ending in "al."

> The skill of the official at the medical hospital,
> Was technical but farcical at best.
> His doctoral demeanor was ethical,
> But comical when put to the test.
> His perpetual bent toward the tyrannical,
> His unusual pastoral sent,
> Made his continual neoclassical lackadaisical behavior,
> Pivotal for his punishment.

➢ **Smack or "Mtcha" sound.** Avoid the habit of starting a story by first making that verbal "mtcha" or "tsk" or "schmack" sound. Keep your mouth slightly open just before speaking so that your involuntary take-in of air will be silent.

> **The best way to learn a new sound is to practice it slowly.** In fact, the secret to speaking English clearly and quickly is practicing slowly and accurately. Here are some words, phrases and paragraphs to use as you exercise. Good luck!

Size and Season
Session and Slash
Musician and Physician
Jazz and Residual

Amidst the mists and coldest frosts,
With stoutest wrists and loudest boasts,
He thrusts his fists against the posts
And still insists he sees the ghosts!

Theophilus Thistle, the successful thistle sifter, in sifting a sieve full of unsifted thistles, thrust three thousand thistles through the thick of his thumb. Now if Theophilus Thistle, the successful thistle sifter, in sifting a sieve full of unsifted thistles, thrust three thousand thistles through the thick of his thumb, see that thou in sifting a sieve full of unsifted thistles, thrust not three thousand thistles through the thick of thy thumb. Success to the successful thistle sifter.

MISUSED AND MISTREATED WORDS AND PHRASES

There is an iconic scene in the satire *Anchorman* when Ron Burgundy, who will read whatever is put in the prompter, signs off by reading a bad word that's been put there by his co-anchor to make Ron look bad. It is a funny scene, but also painfully true. Not that people are sabotaging copy to make anchors look bad. But how many times have I seen an anchor read something live, suddenly realizing afterward that what they read was poor grammar or a mistake or misinformation or a misuse of words.

If you're a writer that likes to get it right, pick up Bill Bryson's book *Bryson's Dictionary of Troublesome Words*. Until then, here are just a few of the common errors I have found during my coaching visits:

> ➢ **Adverse vs Averse.**   *Averse* means reluctant or disinclined. *Adverse* means hostile and antagonistic.

> ➢ **Affect vs Effect.** As a verb, *affect* means to influence or pose. *Effect* means to accomplish.

> ➢ **Aid and Abet.** Redundant.

> ➢ **All intents and purposes.** Redundant and superfluous.

> ➢ **Amoral vs Immoral.** *Amoral* is disregarded morality. *Immoral* is evil.

> ➢ **Anybody and Anyone.** These words are singular and should be followed by singular pronouns and verbs.

> ➢ **Arbitrate vs Mediate.** An arbitrator judges. A mediator negotiates.

> ➢ **The past tense of 'Cast' is 'Cast.'** Not 'casted.'

> ➢ **'Condone' means to pardon, forgive or overlook.** It does not mean to approve or endorse.

> ➢ **"Completely destroyed" and "Totally destroyed."** Both redundant phrases.

> **First and foremost.** Redundant.

> **Hanged vs hung.** People are hanged. Pictures are hung.

> **Opening gambit.** Redundant.

> **I versus Me.** Use "I" as the subject of a sentence and "me" as the object.

> **"She and me will" versus "She and I will."** The correct pronoun is the one that would stand alone in the same sentence. In this case, it would be, "I will."

> **Imply versus infer.** A speaker implies. A listener infers.

> **'Irregardless' isn't a word.** The correct word is *regardless*.

> **Light-year.** This is a measure of distance, not of time. If a planet is a light-year away, its distance from the earth is equal to the distance light travels in one year. One light-year is about 5.88 trillion miles.

> **Stalemate versus standoff.** Stalemates don't end. A chess match that reaches a stalemate is over. Standoffs can be resolved.

> **Who vs Whom**. 'Whom' should be used to refer to the object of a verb or preposition. 'Who' should be used to refer to the subject of a sentence. If you can replace the word with 'he' or 'she,' use 'who.' If you can replace it with 'him' or 'her,' use 'whom.'

Chapter 8

ROMANTIC REALITY

Speak when you have something to say.
Not UNTIL you have something to say.

When I was very young, there was a local children's TV show hosted by 'Ranger Hal' and his sidekick 'Bozo the Clown.' The show would begin at the base of the Ranger's Tower where Ranger Hal would climb down, turn to welcome the kids at home, then introduce cartoons, always beginning with Yogi the Bear. Like the Forest Rangers from *Little Mary Sunshine*, Ranger Hal was clean in soul, body and mind. And Yogi was always a hoot. Loved that bear! Then, in the middle of the half-hour, Ranger Hal and Bozo would welcome a group of children into the studio who had won the opportunity to be the live audience for that day by writing a letter to the station expressing their fervent desires to be on the show. Those interactions with the Ranger and Bozo were magical. Bozo would do slapstick humor and magic with the kids, then Ranger Hal would make everyone an honorary Forest Ranger by handing out official Forest Ranger Badges. I would have given my G.I. Joe Action Soldier and all my Superman comics for just one of those badges. Magical.

So, of course, I started a writing campaign to be on The Ranger Hal Show. Once a week my crayon letters would express dreams of climbing to the top of the Ranger Tower with Ranger Hal, learning magic from this fantastical being called Bozo, and proudly wearing my own Ranger's Badge as I fought forest fires with Yogi. And the day my persistence paid off, when I finally got to walk onto the set of The Ranger Hal show as part of the live studio audience, was the day I discovered the horrible reality about television... that nothing on it was real! The Ranger Tower was nothing more than a six-foot ladder. The 'official' Forest Ranger's Badge was made of tin. And Bozo... well, let's just say this guy must have inspired Stephen King's classic horror film *It*. Stranger Danger, anybody?

If you've been in the broadcast news business for any length of time, none of this is all that shocking to you. In a job that measures success in how 'real' and 'natural' you can come across, it is the most unreal, unnatural job there is. The way you're forced to stand, to sit, the colors you must wear, the make-up and hair you must maintain, IFBs and hand-held mics, green screens and prompters, stilted copy and forced conversations. You might as well be a host at *Disneyland*. I've been a coach in this business for 37 years, and I'm still amazed every time anchors, reporters and weathercasters pull off a show. Every time. Viewers have no idea how difficult it is to do what you do and to do it well. Nor should they.

Romantic Reality is a phrase I coined some years ago to describe the viewers' desire to see 'behind the curtain.' When the show decides to expose a 'real moment,' viewers want that reality, but subconsciously they want it without 'real life' foibles. When the camera sneaks them backstage, viewers want a confirmation of their imagination; that the environment is pristine. During 'real' interactions, they want to get to know who the personalities truly are, but their hope is that they are even better versions of the characters who read them the news. In other words, they want a heightened sense of reality. They want Romantic Reality.

The most basic opportunities we are given to showcase this Romantic Reality are interactions, conducting interviews, post-story Q&As, tosses and takes. Done well, these moments can be interesting and compelling, training your viewers to pay attention whenever you have a 'real' moment or conversation. These moments should ultimately inspire viewers to a loyalty for your persona because you are creating value beyond the content. Done poorly, these moments will disengage the viewers to wait for the next segment or to see what else is on the tube.

IDEAL INTERACTION

Viewers will forget most stories within days or even hours after you've delivered them. However, they will remember a piece of interaction the anchor and weathercaster had about a new puppy, forever! Years after the puppy has passed away, viewers will still walk up to you in the grocery store asking, "So how's that puppy?" It's crazy how powerful interactions can be. I'm sure it has to do with the fact that viewers feel they get a real sense of your character, personality, ideals, and sensibilities during what they think are 'real' moments. Yet, as impressionable these moments are on the viewer, interactions are the least paid attention to by producers and talent when prepping for a show. In fact, most anchors and weathercasters pay no attention to them at all until the moment they are interacting on the air. Which is why so many interactions at the desk are simply inane. This is not only unfortunate, but short-minded and irresponsible.

Ideal Interactions, whether charming and fun or serious and urgent, compel viewers to listen, support the concept that you have value beyond the content, and train viewers to listen in anticipation for your next 'extemporaneous' discussion. So, it's important for the master communicator to know what the elements are that make up Ideal Interaction.

> **Ideal Interaction Elements:**

   ✓ **Concise:** We don't have time for idle chit-chat. Never say two words where one will do. Don't repeat yourself or others. If you have something to say, then say it. But don't ramble. If you have nothing to say, move on!

   ✓ **Confident:** Most interactions drop in energy because no one has a clue, going into them, as to what's going to be said or who's going to say it. When I confront folks about this, the justification is usually that the 'not knowing' keeps it fresh. Which is utter crap. The fact is, if you're on the air, you're being paid to make EVERYTHING you read and say, no matter how many times you've read or said it, sound like it's 'fresh.' Interactions don't need to be scripted, but they do need to be crafted. Choose a theme prior to the interaction and assign a pecking order. Each person should only speak for one beat before the next person picks it up.

   ✓ **Viewer-centric:** Interactions should center around the viewers' interests and concerns, not your own. When they meet you on the street, viewers will tell you how much they liked hearing about your dog or your tomato plants or your drive to work. But, in truth, they couldn't care less. What they want to hear about is THEIR pets and THEIR vegetable gardens and THEIR traffic problems. The bottom line is this, each time you talk about yourself, you run the risk of alienating viewers. It's that simple. As soon as you say, "I took my dog to that event this weekend," you've upset all the cat people. Because cat people think dog people are stuck-up. And dog people think cat people are wimps. Instead, make it about the viewers. Say, "If you're an animal lover, this was a great event to attend!"

In so doing, you've included everyone and alienated no one.

✓ **Substantive:** Too often interaction is built into the show for no apparent reason other than the need to see our people together. Please remember that superfluous interaction hurts the show more than no interaction at all. How many times has a viewer heard a minute of interaction and thought, "You just waisted a minute of my time." It is important to have interaction as long as the content is meaningful to the viewer in some way.

✓ **Moves the Show Forward:** Don't repeat yourself or others. Don't make obvious comments like, "Wasn't that a great story?!?" Of course it was a great story! That's why we put it on the air!! If you are going to speak, say something that progresses the show. Otherwise you're just wasting the viewer's time.

✓ **Avoids One or Two-Word Affirmations:** In the same vain, to move the show forward there's no need to validate the last thing you saw or heard before moving on. To say things like, "That's right!" or "Wow, you're not kidding," is just superfluous, wastes time and stops the flow of the show.

✓ **Active Listening:** Imagine you are one of three people chatting to each other at a party. When one person speaks, the other two will focus their eyes and attention on the person talking. Now imagine that same scenario with one person talking, you are focused on that person talking, but the third person in the group is silently staring at you instead of the person speaking. Awkward, right? And creepy.

Now consider the dynamic with you at the anchor desk with another person. That 2-shot is really a 3-way conversation since the camera is considered the third person. In that case, when the person next to you at the desk is talking, where should you be looking? If we follow the party logic, you should be looking at the person talking! Not staring at the other person (the viewer) who is also listening. Too often the person not talking will be staring into the camera at the viewer instead of looking at the person talking. This can come across as dismissive, uninterested or just like you're waiting to talk instead of being invested in your partner's voice. Always focus on the other speaker before speaking yourself. Your conversation should look like it's been motivated by what you've just heard. The viewer recognizes the difference between listening and waiting to talk.

✓ **Avoids Inside Baseball:** Occasionally anchors will chortle while coming out of a break or a pack, apologizing to the viewers, "Sorry, it's an inside joke." How would you like it if you walked up to a group of friends at a party and they did that to you? You wouldn't because it's exclusionary and rude. The same can be said for humor that spans a break. Don't refer to a quip or joke from a past segment unless you are willing to re-explain the whole thing (not recommended) before moving on.

✓ **Avoids Jokes, Sarcasm and Pranks:** There are daytime viewers who won't watch *The Ellen DeGeneres Show* because Ellen loves to prank her guests; scaring them on national television. These viewers feel that pranks and practical jokes are passive aggressive and mean spirited. *Ellen* is obviously doing quite well in the ratings, so this segment of the of the viewing population is apparently inconsequential to the show. And I would say that if your numbers are so outrageous that you can get away with actions you know will alienate a segment of your viewers, then more power to you. If not, keep in mind that humor is a very subjective thing. What's funny to one person is sacrilegious to another. The practical joke you think hysterical can come across as mean spirited and hateful to others. Other types of jokes to avoid: political, religious, sexual, male versus female, self-effacing, effacing others… you get the picture. It's fine to have a sense of humor about subjects. But using your show as a platform for stand-up comedy only runs the risk of alienating viewers.

✓ **Avoid Physical Contact.** I know this may sound obvious, but keep your hands to yourself during interactions. The moment you make physical contact with the person sitting next to you, even if it's a light tap with your fingers on the top of that person's hand, your relationship suddenly becomes sexualized in the viewer's mind. And that's a distraction nobody wants or needs in broadcast news.

PERSPECTIVE

Viewers don't need you or your show for information. News is a cheap commodity they can find on any local station or with a few quick taps on their devices. However, an element highly valued by your viewer and sorely lacking with many of these sources is perspective. Perspective is the best way to help your viewers understand why they should care about the data or why it's important for them. It isn't just a further description or further information. Perspective makes the story or question or subject more important by siding it up to relative news matters. Perspective is information that makes the subject that much clearer by its presence and given relative to the viewer's reality and sensibilities.

⇒ **News Perspective**:

o A view of the relative importance of things.

o The relationship of aspects of a story to each other and to the whole.

o The capacity to view news items in their true relations or relative importance to other news items or to the entirety of the viewer's reality.

Perspective is not something easily found within the story but more likely what the anchor or weathercaster has accumulated and learned with years of experiencing life, reporting the news and living in the market. Coupled with intelligence and sharply honed skills, perspective is one of the most powerful tools a communicator can wield. And consistency with delivering perspective is a key element for making your persona valuable beyond the content.

Q & A with PERSPECTIVE

One of the best ways to show that you have perspective is with Q&A. When an anchor pops up after the reporter's tag to ask a question and then immediately drops out of sight to hear the answer, it always reminds me of that arcade game Whack-a-Mole. Many times, these pop-up questions feel contrived or 'canned' because our first thought is, "Why didn't the reporter just tell us this information in the first place?" Why did we need this annoying head to pop up and disturb everything? All we want to do is get rid of the nuisance as quickly as possible so that we can get back to the story. Whack-an-Anchor.

Questions preceded by perspective are a whole different matter. In these cases, perspective is grounded in information that could not have easily been obtained at the scene but makes the question that much clearer by its presence. Take for instance the Q&A motivated by a neighborhood shooting story. After the reporter's tag, what we might normally see is the anchor popping up to ask…

ANCHOR: "Was this a gang related shooting? "

… and then just as quickly the Anchor vanishes from sight. It's a stupid question. Why didn't the Reporter just give us that information in the first place? However, if the Anchor pops up and says…

ANCHOR: "I spoke to the police chief earlier today and he tells me that there have been three gang-related shootings in that neighborhood in the last month. Do we know if this was a gang related shooting? "

Suddenly it's an interesting question because the added perspective does three vital things:

First, it gives the question weight; a reason for being asked. The anchor's communication with the police chief uncovered related incidents that motivated the question. We now understand why the anchor would make the interruption to garner this new information.

Second, this perspective tells us something about the anchor. Apparently, he has a strong relationship with the police chief. This gives the anchor more cache with the viewer.

Third, and this is the most important aspect of perspective; whether the viewer cares about this shooting or not, she just learned something about her community she needs to know. Something she probably wouldn't have heard had she been listening to another station because it really wasn't a part of the reporter's story.

In review: Perspective gave the question weight, gave insight to the anchor's persona, and taught the viewer something about the community that she needed to know.

Let's look at another example. This time we're coming out of an elementary school bus crash story. During the report we find out some of the kids on the bus were injured. The anchor pops up to ask the reporter:

ANCHOR: "Was the bus driver able to help those kids? "

The anchor disappears. Another inane question. Why didn't the reporter just tell us? However, if the anchor pops up and asks...

ANCHOR: "At a recent PTA meeting it was discussed that bus drivers are required by law to take a Red Cross course in case of these types of emergencies. Do we know if this bus driver was able to help those kids?"

Again, the perspective here gives the question weight, it tells us something about the anchor (attends PTA meetings so must be a parent) and it teaches the viewer something about the community she needs to know, regardless if she cares about the story.

THE ELEMENTS OF PERSPECTIVE

- ✓ Perspective moves the show forward.

- ✓ Perspective gives insight into the anchor's personal character and journalistic acumen.

- ✓ Perspective teaches something relevant about the news or community.

- ✓ During Q&A, perspective gives the question weight.

  - ▪ It tells the viewer why the question needed to be asked.

  - ▪ It makes the question stronger by siding it up to relative news matters; information the reporter probably wouldn't know.

- ✓ Perspective is viewer-centric. It is best when relative to the viewer's reality, not the anchor's personal experience.

  - ▪ It is okay to begin with a personal experience but should quickly change focus to the viewer.

PREP FOR PERSPECTIVE

Give the show more texture and take it to the next plateau by interjecting perspective into your show. Look at the rundown before heading off to work and start thinking about perspective on your way to work. Identify what stories, intros, tags and Q&A's you could add perspective to if needed. Give the producer options by identifying those areas of opportunity as soon as you get to the newsroom. This process will go a long way toward weaving perspective into every newscast.

Chapter 9

THE ANCHOR

Learn how to fall when it doesn't matter,
So that you can fall with little consequence when it does.

If you believe your job is to show up every day just in time to answer emails, post on social media, natter that the producers never get headlines and teases in on time, check your copy for bad grammar and facts in lieu of sounding like an idiot on the air, grab a bagel, natter that the market is beneath you and that the prompter operator is a moron, put on your make-up, then hit the studio because anchoring is what you do at the end of your day… then chances are, you're not reading this book. Because if it is you, then your career has already stalled out and will eventually flatline at a point far below your potential.

Yes, it is a difficult job. Too much to do and not enough time or staff to do it. It's a miracle that the show doesn't crash-and-burn on any given day. You are a Saint. And not just any Saint. I mean, one of the really good Saints! But unless we run this crawl while you're reading your top stories…

I DESERVE A BIGGER MARKET, A BETTER STATION, A HIGHER SALARY, SMARTER VIEWERS, A HAPPIER SPOUSE, KIDS WHO RESPECT ME, AND A PORSCHE.

...viewers won't know that you could have been digging ditches for a living but instead you sacrificed yourself to anchor the news at this station. Saint!

All joking aside, the anchors I have seen over the years that rise to the top of their markets and their careers have done so by proving to news consumers that they are valuable beyond the content. There is a commonality of elements that these winning anchors all seem to share. Innately or learned, they garner the respect and loyalty of their audiences. In a world where character and individuality are easily pushed aside for a high volume of content and expediency, they have been prudent to note that viewers still thirst for a personal, human condition connection with their anchors.

THE ANCHOR PARADIGM

If you amalgamate all the information from 40 years of research projects, surveys and focus groups answering the question, "What is the perfect anchor?", the result is represented here as the Anchor Paradigm; a very specific skill set the anchor must master in order to build a relationship with the viewer and become dominant in the market. These skills are divided into five levels of growth, each evolving and expanding from the previous level:

THE ANCHOR PARADIGM

LEVEL I: **COSMETIC** – Dress, Make-Up, Appearance, Gestures, Voice Quality, Mannerisms, Body Language.

LEVEL II: **STORYTELLING** – Reading Skill, Diction, Delivery, Clarity, Speed, Smoothness, Copy Interpretation.

LEVEL III: **PROFESSIONALISM** – Personal Style, Naturalness, Interaction Skills, Authoritativeness, Strong Team Leader.

LEVEL IV: **JOURNALISTIC ACUMEN** – Probes, Digs, Investigative, Credibility, Expertise, Knowledgeable, Credentials, Good Writer, Perspective.

LEVEL V: **TRUST** – Charismatic, Friendly, Warm, Comfortable, A Community Asset.

Although each of the levels in the Anchor Paradigm have the same importance for viewers, they are in this order because if LEVEL I isn't mastered, it is very hard for viewers to get past it to appreciate LEVEL II, and so on. For instance, in this paradigm the COSMETIC level is basic to the viewers' acceptance of the anchor. If viewers don't like what they see, it is extremely difficult for them to get past their perception to then listen to what is being said. This isn't a matter of an anchor looking 'pretty' or 'ugly.' It's a matter of looking appropriate for the position. Consider waiting in the examination room to meet your new doctor who suddenly walks in dressed like a jester. No matter how many certificates that doctor has on the wall, it's hard to get past the fact that you're about to be probed by a clown.

This holds true throughout the Anchor Paradigm levels. If one level is missed or not fully realized, the next levels, no matter how well developed, are rendered "null and void" by viewers. To illustrate; consider Level V – TRUST. Without the first four levels, any television personality thought to be a "bubble-head" could also just as easily be considered friendly, warm, comfortable, charismatic and a community asset. It is only when supported by the other four levels of the paradigm that those fifth level characteristics become the highest facets of the anchor. Taken a step further, if viewers have a choice between two anchors who possess the characteristics of LEVELS I thru IV, but only one of those anchors possesses the characteristics in LEVEL V, it is a safe bet that most viewers will choose the latter. The analogy would be choosing between medical doctors. Most people, if given the choice between two doctors who have the exact same educational background and medical experience, would choose the doctor with the best bedside manner.

LEVEL I - COSMETIC

This first level is all about how the audience reacts to the anchor visually. Included here: hair, makeup, clothing, body language and facial expressions. When the viewer accepts the anchor visually, she will move on to...

LEVEL II - STORYTELLING

How the anchor sounds and delivers copy. Is the voice pleasant, easy to listen to and expressive? Is it free of distracting vocal mannerisms? It is smooth, conversational, varietal and inflective along with using the appropriate volume. Is it relaxed and comfortable? If so, the viewer moves on to…

LEVEL III - PROFESSIONALISM

This third level deals with the audience's perception of the anchor as professional. Being comfortable and confident in the anchor role. The viewer perceives the anchor to be a person with an exciting job and an opportunity to contribute to the community. This phase is where the elements of naturalness, authoritativeness, credibility, interaction skills and strong teamwork come into play.

LEVEL IV - JOURNALISTIC ACUMEN

The anchor should be able to show insight and analyze complexity in a way that can be understood. The viewer wants the anchor to be knowledgeable about current events, and deliver helpful perspective regarding the news stories of the day.

LEVEL V - TRUST

The anchor reaches this ultimate level when invited into the viewer's home every day as a trusted friend. At this level, the viewer depends upon the anchor to help her get through the day and improve her ability to cope with the world. Characteristics here are Friendly, Warm, Comfortable, a Community Asset and Charisma. Longevity in a market is a major factor in achieving this phase.

THE COMMAND ANCHOR

If you thought being a 'winning' anchor was enough, think again! Once you have completely immersed yourself in the Anchor Paradigm, to the point that it is synonymous with your on-camera persona, it is time step up to the ultimate challenge few have achieved. Only now can you achieve Command Anchor status. The Command Anchor concept holds that the anchor must be a Gracious Host, the Omniscient Observer, the Viewer's Representative, the Devil's Advocate, the Expert and the Viewer's Protector.

The Gracious Host

The anchor in this role is responsible for making viewers feel comfortable so that they can watch the news and absorb the information without distractions. Unlike the "ringmaster" concept which relegates the anchor to simply introducing one story after another, here the anchor is a true host. The viewer sees the anchor as glad to be on-set doing this job and obviously involved with the material. The anchor must keep the show moving smoothly, cover any gaffs that may occur, handle unforeseen circumstances and make all who appear on-set or in the newscast feel welcome.

The Omniscient Observer

The viewer's perception is that the anchor sees and understands all that takes place during the newscast. In fact, as far as the viewer is concerned, the anchor has a big role in deciding which stories are to be covered and how they are presented. As the Omniscient Observer, the anchor is the 'tie that binds' when it comes to history and context. The anchor understands why any story is important and why the viewer should be listening.

The Viewer's Representative

In reviewing copy before the newscast, the anchor has a specific responsibility to raise the red flag if that copy is confusing or seems to assume knowledge. During the newscast the anchor must listen and understand everything that happens. When questioning a reporter the anchor must do so in a comfortable, layman-like manner because, at this point, the anchor is representing the viewer. The anchor asks questions to clarify those issues important to the viewer. The anchor is the champion of the viewer. The anchor's role is to make sure the flow of information is clear, understandable and well-delivered with energy and commitment. All this must be done in a human, people-oriented style.

The Devil's Advocate

It is important that the anchor play the Devil's Advocate and not the Devil! Rarely should you reveal your own opinion unless you are sure it won't alienate the viewer. Stating that, "I think that teacher was obtuse for doing that!" may not be wrong, but there are many viewers who might feel that the teacher should have the right to due process before being found guilty. Those same viewers will feel alienated by you because of your statement and subsequently find you less credible. Instead, it is more prudent to state that, "Many parents say they feel the teacher was incompetent for his actions." It's the same sentiment, it's the truth, and it takes the onus off you.

The Expert

The Command Anchor knows enough about the subjects that are covered during the show to ask intelligent questions and offer perspective. The Command Anchor is not only well read and wise, but excels to a high degree in two or three main interests, becoming somewhat of an expert in the viewer's mind.

For example: Let's assume the anchor has a strong affinity for children. Becoming a Command Anchor means taking a personal interest in every important children's story the station reports on, being involved in special community services relating to children, promoting and donating time and energy to organizations which help children, owning the station's franchise on children, and adding perspective during the newscast any time a major story breaks regarding children.

As the Command Anchor has expertise in certain subjects, the anchors in a Command Anchor Team complement one another by having different main interests. Together, they have expertise in the major areas of news: crime, health, consumer issues, children's issues, etc. Viewers automatically want to watch the Command Anchor Team whenever a big story breaks because they trust that not only will they receive the data, but they will also gain a better understanding, insight and perspective about the subject and how it relates to their lives, their families and their community.

The Protector

Viewers not only want someone who is going to give them the news, they want a protector. Think about your average viewers. They get up every morning, get dressed, get the kids ready for school, go to work, come home from work, get the kids ready for bed, wind down and go to sleep so they can start all over again the next morning. They don't have time to find out what school districts are doing or not doing for their kids, what neighborhoods are safe to live in or too hazardous to drive through, what they should watch out for as consumers, how to prepare for the coming weather, etc. They need their Command Anchor to protect them. And they will put their faith and loyalty in that anchor for being a demanding investigator, asking the tough questions and getting the needed answers.

HUMAN CONDITION EVENTS LIST

We know for a fact that most people don't physically watch the local news on TV. Instead, they will have it on in the background and listen to it while doing other things like getting ready for work or making dinner. There are a few times however, during a news broadcast, when viewers will stop what they are doing to turn and look at the TV screen. One of those times is at the top of the show or at the top of the halves. Another one of those times is when the anchors toss to weather.

Previously we discussed how Ideal Interaction can mold viewers' perception of your character, personality, ideals, and sensibilities. This means that the toss to weather can be a significant moment if it's well crafted. Unfortunately, most anchors and producers look at the weather toss as nothing more than a hurdle to get from news to the weather segment. Because of this attitude and lack of concern, the viewer gets to hear scintillating exchanges like:

ANCHOR 'A': "It sure is cold out there! Must be, what, 30 degrees? But I know it's going to warm up later this afternoon to, what, in the 40's?"

ANCHOR 'B': "So true! Really cold! Freezing!! And rainy, too! It rained like a lot this morning on my way to work! I'm so thankful it's going to stop raining by this afternoon."

WEATHERCASTER: "You two are so right! Cold and rainy this morning! Really cold and really rainy!"

At this point viewers are ready to shoot themselves. I call this kind of chatter "cracker-barrel conversation" because it does nothing, goes nowhere and is a waste of time. This is the kind of conversation that keeps me away from most parties. And I can tell you that viewers in myriad focus groups over the years have responded, "Just shut up and tell me the weather!"

(As a side note, I can't tell you the number of times over the years weathercasters have pulled me aside and begged me to get the anchors to stop throwing them the weather during the weather toss. They will tell me that half the time the anchors get the weathercast wrong and must be corrected, or the anchors will throw exactly what the weathercaster was going to lead with and now must immediately think of something new to say.)

When throwing to the weathercaster, it isn't the anchor's job to tell us the weather. Oddly enough, that's the weathercaster's job! It's the anchor's job to make the viewer interested in listening to the weathercaster. If you give the weather as a toss, it negates the reason for having a weather person since you obviously already know the weather. Instead of saying, "It's going to rain," say something like, "The Pumpkin Festival is this weekend. Will the weather make it difficult for families to go?" Or say something like, "The leaves are starting to turn on Rout 27 making it such a romantic drive!" Let the viewer know how listening to your weathercaster will enhance her life, live better in her community or help her protect her family.

Anchors usually have a hard time with this because they attempt to come up with something fresh to say at the last minute without any previous consideration and without conferring with the weathercaster. Bad idea on both counts. This is the cause of cracker barrel conversation.

The best way to consistently have great weather tosses is to create a human conditions list that you will be able to refer to all year long. This isn't just a short list of holidays. This would be a list of every local-regional-national event throughout the year affected by the weather. It would include a list of everything KIDS do throughout the year affected by the weather. (That alone is a book: after school events, kid's sporting events, kid's vacations, kid's summer activities, kid's maladies, clothes, etc.) The list would include how people's homes and cars are affected all year long by the weather. And so on. The easiest way to do this is to start a list with four main categories:

EVENTS   KIDS   HOUSE   CAR

Have everyone on the news team add three things to the list each day. Within a month's time, you will have a comprehensive list that will give you something new to throw each-and-every weather hit for the next year that will always be human condition oriented, substantive and viewer-centric. It will make you valuable to the viewer beyond the weather data and worthy of their loyalty.

THE OPEN TOSS

The easiest and most expedient handoff to a reporter in the field is by using a Closed Throw. This is a toss ending with a closed statement or by ending with the reporter's name. A Closed Throw is complete and doesn't require an answer or a response. For example:

> ANCHOR: "Although protesters have been gathering on the courthouse steps, pundits are saying that what we're seeing is nothing more than a knee-jerk reaction to the Mayor's speech. And now we go live to our own Kathy Smith standing in front of the courthouse to tell us more. Kathy?"

There's nothing wrong with the Closed Throw. It does what it's supposed to do, which is direct us to listen to the reporter. But that's all it does. It has no humanity like a conversation, it stops the flow of the show and it makes the Anchor sound like a traffic cop, directing our attention to move quickly. And really, if you think about it, when do you hear someone's name at the end of a sentence in normal conversation between good friends? "I loved the film! How about you... KATHY?!?" I believe the only time we hear a name at the end of a sentence in normal conversation is when we think someone isn't listening or someone is in trouble. "Okay, who took the last cookie?... KATHY?!?"

A much better way to go, in terms of weaving in the human condition, creating a nicer flow and a stronger sense of teamwork, is the Open Throw. An open-ended throw is one that initiates interaction or gives the impression that the reporter is being motivated by what the anchor has just said to continue in the same vain. An open throw can be a question or an open statement. For instance:

> ANCHOR: "Now we go live to our own Kathy Smith, standing in front of the courthouse where protesters have been gathering. And, Kathy, pundits are saying that what we're seeing is nothing more than a knee-jerk reaction to the Mayor's speech."

You'll notice that the content is the same. In fact, the throw is even a bit shorter. All we've done is taken Kathy's name and placed it before the last sentence, making the exchange sound more like a conversation than a command.

The next level would be to make this a Command Anchor throw by adding perspective. We would begin by using whatever information is given by the reporter or written by the producer. Then after Kathy's name, add a bit of perspective, making it more personal and certainly more valuable to the viewer. For instance:

> COMMAND ANCHOR: "Pundits are saying that protesters gathering on the courthouse steps is a knee-jerk reaction to the Mayor's speech. Our own Kathy Smith joins us in front of the courthouse. Kathy, I've received a lot of viewer tweets in the last half hour suggesting these folks are nothing more than a fringe group crying for attention."

THE MEMORABLE MOMENT

When asked about a choice book or film or social event, people will inevitably recount one or two favorite moments that made it so. Most of us are like that when we've seen or experienced something that touched us in some way. So, it is incumbent on the Command Anchor to create at least one memorable moment for the viewer in every show.

Look at the big picture before locking things down and ask, "Is there a memorable moment here? Is there an area of opportunity to create a lasting impression for the viewer?" At the beginning of each day the Command Anchor will look at the rundown to determine what stories are ripe for perspective moments, meet with the producer to go over these areas of opportunity and produce at least one memorable moment in the show. Finding, creating, and delivering that moment on a consistent basis becomes the Command Anchor's signature, and ultimate value to the viewer

THE GRATUITOUS "THANK YOU"

Too often the anchor will use "Thank you" as nothing more than a bridge to get from one thing to the next, uttering it in such an off-handed and absent-minded way that it comes across as by rote, dismissive and insincere.

There are many other ways to make those transitions such as reacting to something the reporter talked about during the segment, adding information, promising follow-up or putting everything in perspective. If for no other reason, replacing the rote "thank you" with something of value highlights the anchor's comments as sincere and much more intelligent.

However, if you want to thank someone, take the beat and look at the person you're thanking directly while you do it. Don't use "Thank you" as a vehicle for scanning your scripts before the next story. Say it if you like, but mean it when you do!

Chapter 10

THE REPORTER

If you are overwhelmed, stop worrying and start doing!
What needs to get done won't be revealed until
you begin to do it!

Being a great reporter is one of the most difficult jobs in TV news. There, I said it! If you're a reporter, you already know this. If you're a layman thinking about getting into the field, just know that a top-notch reporter needs to be a great researcher, interviewer, writer, understand politics, social issues, community issues, grammar, accuracy, proper style, shoot, edit and track packages, develop relationships with contacts and experts for leads and stories, analyze and interpret information, be a skilled communicator, be objective, persistent, have interpersonal abilities, computer skills, stamina for long hours with a high stress level, and be proficient with audio, video and graphics to adapt stories to different social media platforms. There's more, but you get the idea.

My expertise in working with Reporters has mostly to do with developing their communication and storytelling skills to the highest level possible. And I have found with many that this is usually their greatest area of opportunity for growth. Coupled with the deportment, writing and storytelling elements we've already discussed, following are the most common issues I address in Reporter coaching sessions.

THE STAND-UP

Standing in front of a camera and delivering information isn't storytelling. It isn't even news. News isn't news because something happened. Fires, floods, car wrecks, shootings, arrests… these things are not news. They are just things that happen day in and day out. What makes something news is the human condition inherent in the event. A car wreck is just an event until we find out a child was injured in the process. A fist fight isn't significant until we learn that it was between a man and his newlywed. Storytelling isn't about relaying data. It's about zeroing in on the human condition, beginning with that and then weaving it throughout the story.

➤ **The Magazine Cover Lead.** Magazines hook their audience by cover leads that go right to the heart of the story. Four or five words that communicate the human condition of the piece. Consider starting your piece in much the same way. Hook us, then tell us the story. If you promise people the human condition up front, viewer will want to take the ride.

➤ **Work with your environment.** Appeal to the viewer's senses. The most important thing about being live is to make the viewer feel like she is there. When possible, give viewers a real sense of what it's like at the scene. Reference surroundings, conditions, mood, etc. Relate the firsthand experience. Better yet, be a part of the environment as opposed to standing in front of it. Touch a mailbox. Talk to a bystander. Be affected by the surroundings. The viewer can't be there. Your job is to make the viewer taste it, touch it, smell it, feel it, and experience it through you.

➤ **Don't repeat the anchor's throw to you.** In normal conversation, we rarely repeat the last thing someone said to us before we start talking. Repetition also softens the edge, kills urgency and is disengaging to the ear.

➤ **"That's (not) right!"** There's no need to begin your stand-up validating the anchor by saying, "That's right", after the throw to you. Rarely in life do we continue a conversation we're having with a friend by saying, "That's right." Also, if you make a habit of doing so, it begins to sound by rote and insincere. Instead, your response should sound like it was motivated by what you've just heard and at the same time move the show forward.

➤ **Nod to validate.** You should be communicating even before you begin to speak. It's perfectly fine to add a little nod of the head when the anchor is throwing to you. Just don't overdo it. In life we nod occasionally while someone is speaking to us as validation, so it is perfectly acceptable and natural.

➤ **Morning Nuggets.** I know it isn't easy to do a thousand hits in the morning and make them all fresh. One trick that helps is to remember that all your content doesn't all have to reflect present time. Adding sidebar facts to supplement the material so that you are not repeating the same information in the exact same way will make your hits more interesting to your viewer and to yourself.

➤ **Perspective can keep things interesting.** Perspective isn't just a further description or information. Rather, it makes the story or question more important by siding it up to relative matters. Perspective gives clarity by its presence.

➤ **Dress for the environment.** It's hard for viewers to concentrate on your story if you look like you're out of place. A suite is appropriate when standing in front of a courthouse.

Not so much when standing in the middle of a pig sty. Doing so will make the viewer think about your appearance, not the story. Whenever possible, wear clothes appropriate to the environment. Many reporters keep clothes variations in their car just in case a quick change is in order.

➤ **I think; therefore, I am… NOT.** Stay away from the phrase, "I think." What you think is not relevant. What you know based on your background, years of experience, knowledge from the data you've collected and the people you've talked to is what matters and why you are there.

➤ **Push yourself to be creative!** If the scene is the dark side of a brick building, find another way. Reporting on a vote by the school board to put seatbelts in school busses could be done in a school bus. Reporting on the arrest of a thirteen-year-old boy jacking cars could be done in a teenager's den playing Grand Theft Auto with his friends.

➤ **Open Ended Toss-backs.** Signing off at the end of a piece, "I'm Jane Smith live in front of this building, now back to you in the studio," is impersonal, kills teamwork, and slows the pace of the show. The reporter's toss back to the anchor should be as open as the anchor's toss was (hopefully) at the beginning of the piece. An open-ended toss back to the anchor is one that initiates interaction or give the impression that the anchor is being motivated by what the reporter has just said to continue in the same vain. For example:

> REPORTER: "…and although the fire has been raging on for days, (Anchor's name), the Chief tells me there is no end in sight."

Notice that the reporter uses the anchor's name just before ending the piece. This alerts the anchor and production that the reporter is throwing back. The anchor's first words would be in response to that thought, which would then lead to Q&A, or back into the rest of the show.

➢ **Avoid the Roll Cue Ending.** The "Roll Cue Ending" is a phrase I created to describe the unnatural delivery style sometimes used by anchors and reporters to signify the end of a story; moving on to the next segment or cuing production to roll tape. It begins with a dramatic pause just before uttering the last two or three words. Although the Roll Cue Ending can be effective, it must be remembered that it is a storytelling device not found in day-to-day conversation. Therefore, if it is overused, it becomes distracting and sounds insincere.

➢ **Your viewer's ear is only six inches away.** Sometimes it feels like the reporter is yelling at the camera because, well… they are yelling at the camera. I know it's difficult when you're in the thick of it to remember that you don't necessarily have to talk over ambient sound or to hit the camera with your voice. Your viewer's ear is as close as your handheld.

➢ **Hope for the best, prepare for the worst.** If you start your live shot with nothing more than explaining the scene, you can come across as stiff or cavalier. When going to the scene, hope that the environment will give you something to work with, but be prepared for nothing more than a brick wall. What will you say or do to make that brick wall interesting? What will you do to begin with a memorable moment?

➢ **It's okay not to have an answer.** There will be occasions when anchors will ask questions and you simply don't know the answers. Don't be thrown. It's their job to ask questions they think the viewer would want answers to, whether you have those answers or not. The best response is to be honest and promise a follow-up answer if it's likely to be available.

➢ **Explain it so that your audience can relate to it.** Occasionally it's a good idea to convert facts you got from the source into language the viewer understands. For example, after reporting that a man fell 100 feet to his death, that distance might mean more to the viewer if you then explained that 100 feet is about the same height as a ten-story building. Other examples:

  o An acre of land is about the size of a football field.

  o 70 mph wind is close to hurricane level conditions.

  o One inch of rain falling on one acre of ground (a football field) is equal to about 27,000 gallons of water and weighs about 113 tons.

  o An inch of snow falling evenly on one acre of ground (a football field) is equivalent to about 2,800 gallons of water.

IN STUDIO

➢ **Don't blow-off the anchor during the introduction.** Don't be too anxious to get to the prompter. Make sure you are actively listening instead of waiting to talk. Eye contact should be strong and your interaction with the anchor should be true. Finish a beat, thought, or phrase with the anchor before going to the viewer. Don't make the viewer feel like you're rushing to get out of the conversation so that you can get to your piece. Make it look like you're invested in your relationship with the anchor and in the conversation. There is a "halo effect" when you do this well. If viewers like the anchor and it looks like the anchor has a strong affinity for you and your craft, then the viewers will like you as well.

➢ **Why are you standing at the monitor?** If it's being used as an OTS graphic, then your full address should be to the viewers. However, if there are compelling pictures or video running behind you, use it to support your story by indicating when appropriate.

THE PACKAGE

Of course, your goal is to produce a package that includes great video, characters, facts, plot twists and a climax. However, a paradigm of the average story looks something like this:

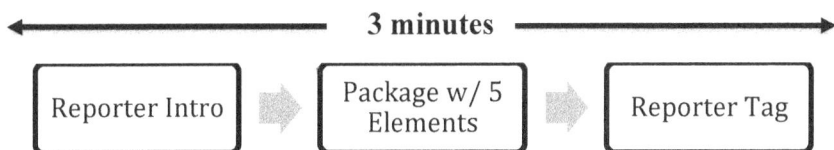

◄——— 3 minutes ———►

| Reporter Intro | ⇨ | Package w/ 5 Elements | ⇨ | Reporter Tag |

This might be necessary if the package must live on its own over a variety of platforms. However, it should be noted that viewers can only process so much information in one package and tend to disengage if there are more than three elements presented. Therefore, it would be better to spread out those elements throughout the paradigm. Use one element for an Anchor/Reporter interaction, use 3 elements for the package and then have another element during an Anchor/Reporter debrief or Q&A.

← ──────────────── **3 minutes** ────────────────→

| Anchor Reporter 1 Element | → | Reporter Intro | → | Package 3 Elements | → | Reporter Tag | → | Anchor Reporter Q&A |

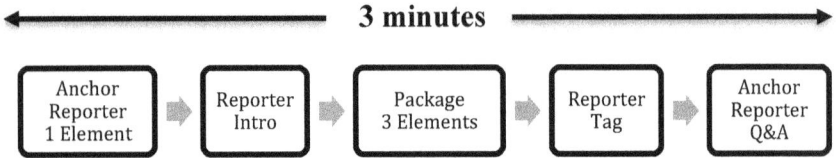

Many reporters tend to look on interactions with anchors at the beginning and ends of their segments as hurdles they must jump in order to do their real jobs. This is a mistake since viewers believe the segment has begun the moment they see the reporter on camera. Make these interactions impactful and use them to your advantage. Consider practicing Ideal Interaction.

➢ **Watch and listen with the viewer's eyes and ears.** After living with a story all day, it's easy to cut a piece together based on your perceptions instead of the viewer's actual knowledge. Before locking a piece down, take a final look and listen as the viewer. Make sure she totally understands the piece and that all her questions have been answered.

➢ **Complete the circle.** One dynamic storytelling device is to end the story by completing something you started at the beginning of the piece. Examples would be answering a question posed at the beginning, solving a conundrum created at the beginning or showing a change with you, another character or the environment now that we've all lived through your piece.

➢ **Find the human element of each story.** Don't just interview the police or investigators. Instead of just using sound bites from official spokespeople, find the person-effected side of the story. The viewers can relate better to a story if a reporter takes the human angle.

➢ **Storyboard your packages.** The best way to have great material coming out of a shoot is having great ideas going into one. Whenever possible, come up with several scenarios in your head or on paper before talking to the photog. Go in knowing what material you'll need to make your story compelling.

➢ **Avoid starting from a dead stop.** When recording a look-live walk-and-talk, the natural inclination is to stand on one's mark, count down out loud from three, begin speaking, and then walk. The problem with this is that the edit must include a 'dead beat' at the beginning to capture your first word. A better technique is to start walking before you begin to speak so that the beat prior to your first word has life.

➢ **Why are you counting yourself down?** When dinosaurs ruled the Earth and packages were shot on film, reporters would count themselves down, "In five… four… three… two…" before saying their first words because the audio track was recorded separately from the film track and the two had to be matched and spliced together in postproduction before air.

In today's world of boxed wine and shake weight dumbbells, there's no need to count yourself down. In fact, doing so takes you out of the feeling and tone you should have just before speaking. Instead of counting, spend your energy before the moment getting into the moment.

TRACKING

➢ **Your track should sound as conversational as your live work.** Both should be urgent, immediate, and fresh. To do this you must first be specific about the identity of the viewer you're talking to (42, female w/ kids, etc.). Remembering that tone of voice (emotional tones) is the single strongest vocal communicator, take note of the emotional tones and coloration's in that story and in those sentences. Break them down to the essential human condition words and phrases most important to that female viewer, and then decide what emotional tones you should attach to those human condition words and phrases.

➢ **To help you decide how each sentence should sound,** begin by printing the entire script without SOTs so that it reads like a narrative. Practice it out loud as a complete story so that you hear the differences between the lines. Then use what you've learned while recording the individual tracks.

➢ **Approximate all the communication elements you use in a live shot when tracking.** What makes delivery conversational is more than manipulating the voice. Conversational delivery is a mixture of speech, vocal variety, facial expressions, body language, focusing on the person you're talking to and concentrating on communicating the human condition.

BREAKING NEWS

➢ **Develop your Breaking News skills.** The best way to develop your ability to be cohesive, concise, and colorful with your delivery of breaking news is practice. First, read a newspaper or magazine article. During that read make mental notes of your intro, two main concepts or ideas you will deliver, an added piece of your own perspective and a tag. Next, using a camera or audio device to record your delivery, present those five elements as you would in a live presentation. Be as concise as possible and use as much vocal variety as possible in the same amount of time you would normally be given for the segment. Listen to what you've done then do it a second time with corrections.

➢ **Journalize:** Preparation is everything for the spot-news reporter. Keep a journal of all the 'evergreen' facts you learn about a subject when you report. Especially natural disasters. As time goes on you will have a lot of useful information already at your fingertips that you can pull from your journal when going into a 'new' situation. This will allow you to use perspective as soon as you arrive on the scene without having to speak to an official if one isn't available. The Journal will also help with Q&A.

ODDS AND ENDS

➢ **Anchor questions** need to make use of the eyewitness reporter's ability to describe what can be seen, heard, smelled, tasted, or felt.

➢ **Tell the viewer the story.** Use the anchor or reporter's name only in tosses. A name may be used in a take if the single sentence is directed to that single person.

➢ **Furnish or help produce a strong lead.** If the intro isn't compelling, the viewer won't stay around for the story.

➢ **Be the eyewitness.** Viewers expect firsthand, "eyewitness" detailed presentations. The eyewitness material should be the meat of the reporter's package: firsthand facts; colorful involved narrative; emotional or "for the record" sound bites from those involved; and creative on-the-scene stand-ups, bridges, and cutaways.

➢ **Have a good reason for doing them.** Viewers say they see no value in live shots done simply for the sake of "going live," or stand-ups that don't have a clear purpose.

➢ **Show and tell!** Showing something, demonstrating something, is the most effective element in a live shot or stand-up. It's inherently interesting; it defines the purpose of the live shot or stand-up; it involves the reporter in the story.

➢ **Narrate video.** Tell viewers who and what they're seeing. Flesh out your narration with comments related to the video. For instance, "Now, the man you see there in the middle is Johnson. Police think he's the one who actually pulled the trigger...."

➢ **Care about the story.** You must believe a story is important before you can convince viewers of it. Don't worry about being slick and polished. Be convincing and be prepared. The bottom line: Never expect a listener's level of caring to exceed your own.

➢ **Use movement to control viewer attention.** Let the viewer know where you want her to look by indicating, then talking to the camera.

➢ **Remember the ten-second rule.** Every ten seconds the viewers need a reason to continue to watching your story. That means sound bites, stand-ups and each audio track should be no longer than ten seconds in length. Natural sound is a good tool to help break-up a long audio track.

Chapter 11

THE WEATHERCASTER

If you hit the bull's eye every time, you're standing too close
to the target. It is challenge that makes us.

I want to ride my bike later today so I just checked my
phone. Apparently, it'll be sunny and 86 degrees by 2pm, which
is perfect.

That whole operation took me about seven seconds.
Seven! So why do I need you? Yeah, yeah… if I wait a few hours
to see you on the news, you're going to tell me why all the
conditions that have already taken place, took place. And then
you'll tell me what's probably going to happen for the rest of the
day and the week and why. But we're living in an immediate
gratification world. Do I really want to wait? Or should I just go
on line right now and get my seven-day forecast? A four second
operation, at best.

"YES! You should wait!" you demand… pleasantly.
Then you go on to argue that my consideration should include the
mountains of education and training you endured to understand
and utilize higher mathematics, advanced physics, chemistry and
computer technologies to bring me the most accurate information
possible. And that it takes a good amount of skill to accurately
read models, forecast conditions, put together segments, shoot and
edit weather material, develop graphics, build shows, and ad lib at
the desk and key wall so that it looks and sounds conversational,
but at the same time professional. Then you enthusiastically shout

out, "You can't get all of THAT on a quick seven-day internet graph! Right?!?"

Well, yes, of course you're right. Unfortunately, all that, plus $150 bucks, might buy a decent steak dinner at the Capital Grille in Chicago. But it won't get me something I can't get on any other local news channel in the market. In the viewer's mind, these attributes are now standard requirements for today's Weathercaster. And viewers don't give credit for the basics. What they want is… well, you guessed it, VALUE BEYOND THE CONTENT!

WEAVING THE HUMAN CONDITION

Determined to bolster viewership, The Weather Channel took me on as their talent coach from 2000 – 2009. At that time research suggested that, although they were doing great with delivering the weather, they could do better connecting with and holding on to their viewers. When I first looked at the product, I determined that most of the OCMs (On Camera Meteorologists) were dynamite at the science, but spent little or no time weaving the human condition into their presentations.

Each time I would have a first session with one of the many OCMs, I would ask the same question, "Why did you chose Meteorology as a profession?" In almost every instance I would get a similar answer. It seems that most weathercasters have been fascinated with weather conditions from the time they were children. That fascination eventually turned into a love that became a lifelong passion. And passion is, after all, a human condition. Right?

Which is why they were baffled when I would suggest during those sessions that their ratings would improve if they would produce shows that offered more than just weather conditions.

"But," they would reply, "We're The Weather Channel."

"I am aware," I would say.

"Isn't that why viewers tune in? For the weather?" They would explain, as if I were a child, "We ARE the WEATHER Channel!"

"I get it," I would say, "But it's hard for people to process so much data without the human condition attached to it."

At this point defenses would begin to emerge.

"Weather conditions ARE human conditions," they would assure me, rather pointedly.

"No, weather conditions have no human condition unless you attach human conditions to them," trumping their point.

"OUR viewers would disagree!" As if I were a child raised by wolves.

"Only because YOUR viewers are weather geeks!"

Okay, I probably shouldn't have said that. In fact, we all know I just stepped over the line.

Trying to recover, "Which is fine. Some of my best friends nerd out on the weather."

Nope. Only dug the hole deeper. But I would continue, undaunted.

"Look, shouldn't we be trying to cast a wider net?" (After all, that's why I'm here.) "Like for, you know, regular people?!?" Okay, apparently, I really can't help myself.

At this point it was always a good time to throw in a little logic. Weathercasters love logic. Right?

"Let me ask you this," I would say, "What's the human condition of rain?"

"Viewers love the rain," they would say, "It cleans the air and helps things grow! Ha!! THAT'S a human condition!" As if I had been trapped.

"True," I would reply, "but what about the viewers who live in a flood plain?"

Suddenly they would have a shift in tone, "Rain could be a problem for those people."

"Exactly!" Pouncing, as if I really had been raised by wolves. "Rain has no human condition unless we attach a human condition circumstance to it.   The same with temperatures. Temperatures in-and-of themselves have no human condition unless they are attached to something that does.   Fifty degrees to people living in Canada means something completely different than fifty degrees to people living at the equator."

Lights begin to dawn.   Defenses begin to lower.

Riding on that tide of agreement, I would finish with, "When you attach human conditions to weather conditions, viewers not only have a better understanding of the information but tend to remember it longer.   And then it becomes easier to apply it to their daily lives."   Knowing better, but blurting out anyway, "Even for nerds."

I still have quite a few friends at The Weather Channel. Go figure.

Once the idea of connecting human conditions to weather conditions made sense to the OCMs, my next hurdle was to convince them of the impossible.   For this newfangled approached to work, human conditions needed to be woven throughout the shows.

"Throughout the shows?!? You do realize our shows are sometimes three hours long," Explaining to the wolf boy.

"Yep."

"And you're suggesting we weave the human condition that whole time," Thinking I would realize my horrible mistake and would quickly recant.

"Yep."

"Just to be clear, how much time is the 'whole time'?" They would ask.

"The brain likes to be stimulated every ten to fifteen seconds," I would say, matter-of-factly.

"So," making sure I understood English, "Every TEN to FIFTEEN seconds."

"YES!" Happy that the concept was finally understood, received and accepted.

"HAHAHAHAHAHAHAHAHAHAH!"

Okay, maybe not accepted… yet. However, I would like to believe that response was an expression of love and respect, as opposed to sarcasm and cynicism. Hope springs eternal.

Of course, their concern was valid. How were these folks supposed to come up with enough human conditions to weave through an entire hour, much less three or even four? Much of which was improvised. Well, necessity being the mother of invention, this is the quandary that led me to invent the 'Events List' (described in Chapter 8) for my Weather Channel comrades.

HUMAN CONDITION PERSPECTIVES

Consistency with adding human condition perspectives to your interactions or key wall presentations takes more than positive thinking. That will only result in hit-and-miss performances. And considering the human condition at the last-minute, just before an interaction or walking in front of the key, will result in repeating the same old clichés' like, "Take that umbrella!" or, "Dress in layers!"

➢ **Planning and pre-show preparation is vital.** Create a human conditions list that you can refer to all year long. This isn't just a short list of holidays. This should be a list of every local-regional-national event throughout the year affected by the weather. It should include a list of everything KIDS do throughout the year affected by the weather: after school events, kid's sporting events, kid's vacations, kid's summer and winter activities, kid's maladies, kid's attire, etc. The list should include how people's homes and cars are affected all year long by the weather. And so on. This comprehensive list will allow you to always add human conditions that are fresh, viewer centric, and appropriate. It will allow you to be of value to the viewer beyond the weather data.

➢ **Hero with a thousand faces.** There are many ways to weave the human condition into your presentations besides utilizing the above events list.

   o **Put weather conditions into perspective.** You can say, "Those winds will get up to 70 miles an hour. That's close to hurricane level status." Other perspective examples:

      ▪ **30 feet** is about the same height as a three-story building.

      ▪ **An acre of land** is almost as big as a football field.

      ▪ **One inch of rain** falling on one acre of ground is equal to about 23,000 gallons of water and weighs about 113 tons.

      ▪ **An inch of snow** falling evenly on one acre of ground is equivalent to about 2,800 gallons of water.

   o **Mention landmarks, mascots, favorite public hangouts, etc.** This has the added benefit of giving the viewer the perception that you are a member of the community as well.

- o **Personify weather conditions**. You can give weather conditions human (or even animal) characteristics. Using words like "tease," "dance," "jump," and "clobber," can add color and energy to your delivery.

- o **Attach emotional tones to weather conditions.** Saying the word "snow" in a happy tone can indicate playfulness. Saying it in a dire tone can indicate that it will be dangerous.

➤ **Next, consider human conditions when building your key wall presentations.** If you've built ten graphs, before you walk away, take a look at the human conditions list that you've created and choose a few to weave into your presentation. Make the decision that human conditions will be part of your weather story at that point instead of it being an afterthought while you're on the air.

AREAS OF OPPORTUNITY

My work with Weathercasters develops their communication skills, connecting with the viewers to the highest level, not only in front of the key but with interactions, writing teases, producing packages, performing live shots, etc. Along with the deportment, writing, and storytelling elements we discussed in previous chapters, following are the most common issues I address in Weathercaster coaching sessions.

➤ **Variety is the spice of life.** Most Weathercasters fall into the bad habit of repeating a crutch phrase like, "Right now," or "As you can see," throughout their segments. Crutch phrases weaken the message and can also disengage the viewer's ear.

Be vigilant against using crutch phrases by reviewing airchecks.

➢ **Strengthen your teases.** This isn't a time for idle chatter. If you happen to be in a growing market, you have new eyeballs looking at you every day. To gain new viewers, you need to hook them immediately. Make sure the first four words of your teases do exactly that! Don't talk about the past unless it is compelling. Stick with present and future conditions that support your weather story. Be compelling and be urgent.

➢ **Brevity is the soul of wit.** Don't overproduce yourself. There's an old broadcast maxim that goes, "Write short, read long." If the words take every second just to be uttered at their fastest, you leave yourself no time to color the words with greater meaning. The viewer would rather experience eight graphs explained well than 15 graphs speeding by so fast the words or concepts get lost. If you have a minute, produce for 50 seconds, then take a minute to say it.

➢ **Don't assume the viewer is watching your weathercast.** Remember that the viewer is mostly listening instead of watching. Therefore, how you tell the story is just as important as the graphics that are on the wall behind you. Remember that graphic transitions should usually be accompanied by story transitions. In other words, when the graphics change from Tuesday to Wednesday, or when we flip to a day-part or 7-Day graphic, it is a good idea to give the viewer the message verbally as well; "And now on to your extended forecast…" If you throw up a graphic and don't mention that you've moved on from the last graphic or mention at least one data point on the new graphic, there's a good chance the viewer won't know that it's up. Be as visual with words as you are with your graphics.

➢ **Your facial expressions and tonality should match the message.** Smiling while talking about severe weather can make you appear cavalier or insensitive to your viewer's plight. Be amiable when appropriate. But matching the right facial expressions and tonality to weather conditions will garner a better understanding and respect.

➢ **Don't repeat a human condition within the half hour.** Once you've said "umbrella" or "dress the kids warm" then you shouldn't repeat that sentiment for the rest of the show. Any form of repetition is disengaging for the ear making it harder for the viewer to continue listening.

➢ **Build lists.** The statement "rain, hail, and tornados" is different than the phrase "tornados, hail, and rain." The distinction should be evident, not only in the structure, but in the vocal build and tonal emphasis placed on each word. Whether your list is a group of words or a succession of sentences, they need to be delivered with a gradient or with variety.

➢ **The 80% versus 20% rule.** Occasionally I'll poke fun at weathercasters by suggesting they only feel like coming to work when there is activity. When it's blue skies and fair sailing, they don't want to get out of bed. However, it is important to remember that your viewer feels the exact opposite. She WANTS to know when there's great weather so that she can live her life and plan activities for her family. And since 80% of your weathercasts are about uneventful days, it is vital that you use these opportunities to gain your viewer's trust and demonstrate that you're the one they are going to want to watch when severe weather strikes. This means showing her that you have value beyond the content.

➢ **Pace vs. Rate.** Rate is the speed of delivery, how fast the weathercaster speaks. Pace is the ebb and flow of your storytelling, including pauses, intense passages and the full range of dramatic relief. Most weathercasters lose their pace when they push their speaking speed past their natural limits. They also lose meaning, intensity, interpretation and emotional range. They swallow words; they skip periods. Use effective pauses, phrasing and vary the tone of your weather stories.

➢ **Don't dwell on the past or other areas of the country.** Remember why your viewers watch (or listen) to you. If it doesn't immediately affect their lives, they don't much care. They're watching you because they need to plan for their lives and to keep their families safe. Give them what they want. Make it local; with an emphasis on the present and the future.

➢ **On the other hand,** if you want to take us to another part of the country, make sure you let us know why we should care BEFORE we go there. Since we know viewers will disengage if it isn't local (or if they think it won't affect them), tell them up front how it may affect them in the future. The exception to this rule is talking about severe weather that is or has tragically affected a people or a region.

➢ **Train your brain to self-edit.** Impromptu speech is an artform that must be practiced for consistency. Improvisation can lead to being long-winded and repetitive if not checked. Try this at home: Pick a concept and take two minutes to explain it out loud. Take the same concept and do it again in one minute. Then again in 30 seconds. Exercise your brain to

self-edit three or four times each week for a few months until
the sharpened skill finds its way into your presentations.

➢ **Six degrees of separation.** When you need to buy time and
faced with a graph of several towns with similar temperatures,
instead of saying, "It's 72 in Smithville, 74 in Greenville, 76
in Brownsville," etc. Truncate the delivery by saying, "It's in
the seventies in Smithville, Greenville, and Brownsville."

➢ **Approachability verses Strength.** Severe weather market
viewers want a weathercaster that is both approachable and
strong. Someone they feel comfortable walking up to on the
street, but at the same time someone who will protect them
during severe weather. Most weathercasters have the
approachability thing down. Usually, the biggest area of
opportunity seems to be weaving the element of strength into
everyday weathercasts. It isn't enough to wait for severe
weather to show how you handle it. You must train the viewer
daily that when severe weather occurs, you will be the one to
watch. Many times, this can be done by adding just a touch of
science to demonstrate that you are an expert or cutting out
conditional words in your lexicon.

➢ **Avoid conditional phrases when they are superfluous.** Be
assertive! Conditional words like, "pretty much," and
"maybe," can weaken your message and dissipate your energy.
For example:

CONDITIONAL	UNCONDITIONAL
"It's a pretty nice day."	"It's a nice day."
"It's kinda cloudy."	"It's cloudy."
"Some scattered clouds."	"Scattered clouds."
"Could be potentially significant."	"Potentially significant."

➤ **Stay in the shot.** It's very distracting to have only part of your body in the shot while in front of the key. Utilize both sides of the key so that you can stay in the shot as often as possible.

➤ **Don't fidget with that clicker.** At the desk it makes you look nervous and at the wall it is just plain distracting. Any kind of superfluous movements only dissipates your energy and weakens your presentation. Use those hands to support your communication.

➤ **"Unbelievable!"** Be careful of using hyperbole like, "What you're about to see is unbelievable," or "It literally rained cats and dogs." Over time, this kind of exaggeration can mare credibility.

➤ **Stay away from colloquialisms such as "ya know," and "I mean."** It's difficult when you're impromptu, but too many colloquialisms will diminish your message and erode your credibility. Practice every day by challenging yourself to get through entire phone calls or conversations without using "ya know" or "I mean." In a relatively short period of time this process will eradicate those superfluous phrases from your daily speech as well as your on-air presentations.

➤ **Three-shots don't need to be longer, just smarter.** Too often three-shots can seem too long because the anchors don't say anything yet take an inordinate amount of time to do it. Instead of saying the same thing three times…

> ANCHOR A: "Wind can certainly hinder travel."
> ANCHOR B: "Yes, it sure can!"
> WEATHERCASTER: "Boy, you said THAT right!"

…we can spend the same amount of time moving the show along by substantive interaction,

> ANCHOR A: "Travel can be affected by strong winds."
> ANCHOR B: "In fact, wind shear is one of the top three weather conditions that delay flights."
> WEATHERCASTER: "Which is happening right now at the airport."

➤ **Again and again and again.**   Avoid using phrases like "Again," or "As I said earlier," when transitioning to another map or another concept during your key wall presentation (or any time for that matter). It is a disengaging word to the ear and for the subconscious because it suggests that you are being redundant. Your job is to repeat yourself. Just don't tell the viewer you're doing so. Find a different way to say it!

➤ **Help the anchors with their throws to you.** Ensure that you have a great springboard into your segment by giving the anchors an appropriate toss.

➤ **Tell us where we're going before you take us there.** Consider days of the week as human conditions. It is so much more effective and dynamic to tell the viewer what day of the week will be affected before relaying what the conditions will occur on that day. This is especially true when changing graphics.

➢ **I think, therefore I am... NOT.** Stay away from phrases like, "I think," or "I guess," when forecasting. What you think is not relevant. What you know based on your background, years of experience, knowledge, and ability to read models and extrapolate from patterns is what's important. It may seem like a thin line, but saying something as simple as, "It looks like rain," sounds so much better than, "I think it's gonna rain."

➢ **I won't dance, so don't ask me!** Perpetual motion when in front of the key dissipates the message. Control that energy and only move when you are making a point. In this way, your presentation will be stronger.

➢ **A one-quarter stance (or 'First Position') at the key wall is strong and probably the most versatile.** Showing your profile and back are weak body positions. Your key work will be stronger if you can stay somewhat open to the viewer during the entire presentation. A one-quarter stance allows you to indicate weather conditions on the map while remaining open to the viewer.

A WORD ABOUT THE 7-DAY GRAPHIC

How important would you say a forecast graphic like the 3-Day or 5-Day or 7-Day is within the context of your weather segment? I know what your viewers would say. I'm pretty sure you know as well. The forecast is THE most important thing to them. If they had to choose one thing out of everything that you present to them, it would be the forecast or 7-Day graphic. And yet, how many times have I seen weathercasters speed through that graphic or drop it completely because they just ran out of time. Could you imagine going to a doctor for a malady, having the doctor run all the tests and explain to you exactly what you have and how you came to have it, but just before telling you how to cure the problem, the doctor suddenly steps out of the exam room never to return. Frustrating, right? That's exactly how your viewer feels when you short-shrift the 7-Day graphic.

Do yourself and your viewers a favor. Follow these three rules when producing your major weather segment:

1) **Give your 7-Day graphic the time it deserves.** Figure out how much time your viewers need to review the 7-Day Graphic (I would suggest at least 15 seconds) and back-time your segment so that (barring severe weather) the 7-Day always gets its due.

2) **Always announce the 7-Day graphic as it appears.** Remember, your viewer is listening more than she's watching. If she misses the seven-day, she'll look it up on her phone. And if she's relegated to doing so, you will have no value to her. Say what you need to say ("Here's your 7-Day forecast" or "Let's take a look at your next 7 days," or whatever…) every time as soon as it appears to give the viewer ample opportunity to stop what she's doing and look at the TV screen.

3) **Weave in the human condition!** Since we know that viewers pay close attention to this graphic, it is the perfect opportunity to show that you have her sensibilities while presenting in front of it.

HARD WRAP

*The great artist learns technique for support,
and then abandons to fly dangerously close to the sun.*

It's simple, really. To be a great communicator, it is vital to understand the human condition; how it affects your target audience and how to use that knowledge when you create, write and deliver. You must also base your development, your focus on performance, and the very nature of your public persona, on the ideal that it's not about you. It's all about the audience.

As an anchor or weathercaster, it is your job to act as the parent, the doctor, the leader and the protector. The success of your broadcast news career is dependent on your ability to give the viewer the perception that you will always be there to help her protect her family, live better in the community, and enhance her life. And if you're not that person now, the hope is that through learning the concepts and performing the exercises contained in these chapters, behavior modification (the constant repetition of doing a thing that is foreign to you until it becomes natural to you) will prevail.

We've gone over quite a bit of material that can't all be processed, absorbed and mastered quickly. So, it is important to prioritize. Consider choosing an area of opportunity to focus on first and develop that for a while before moving on to the next. The concepts to master first because they are the support for what follows are:

- VOICE (Chapter 6)
- SPEECH (Chapter 6)

- WRITING (Chapter 4)
- BODY LANGUAGE (Chapter 2)
- UNDERSTANDING THE TARGET VIEWER (Chapter 3)
- PREPARING AND INTERPRETING COPY (Chapter 5)

Once you're well on your way with those, it's time to really pay attention to the areas of...

- PERSPECTIVE (Chapter 7)
- HIGH CONCEPT (Chapter 4)
- IDEAL INTERACTIONS (Chapter 7)
- THE ANCHOR PARADIGM (Chapter 8)

When I was a kid, my parents would always tell me that, "With hard work, persistence, moral values and a great attitude, you can achieve great things!" Since then, during my lifetime, there have been quite a few changes on the planet. Personal computers, DNA testing and sequencing, electric cars, fiber optics, non-invasive laser and robotic surgery, solar energy, bar codes and scanners, coronary bypass surgery and stents, smart phones, online shopping, the microwave oven, the world wide web, ATMs, GPS, and MRIs. But one thing remains the same. With hard work, persistence, moral values and a great attitude, you can achieve great things.

~ Carpe Diem ~

GLOSSARY

ACTIVE VOICE: The receiver of the verb's action follows the verb, i.e., *"The hungry lion bit the man."* The simple formula for writing in the active voice is, NOUN – VERB – OBJECT.

ANCHOR PARADIGM, THE: A very specific skill set the anchor must master in order to build a relationship with the viewer and become dominant in the market. These skills are divided into five levels of growth, each evolving and expanding from the previous level. The five levels are: 1) COSMETIC, 2) STORYTELLING,   3)   PROFESSIONALISM,   4) JOURNALISTIC ACUMEN, 5) TRUST.

AUXILIARY VERBS: Also known as Helping Verbs are forms of the verbs, "be," "do," "have," and "will," when followed by another verb in order to form a question, a negative sentence, a compound tense, or the passive. Helping verbs tend to weaken the message and should be avoided when writing headlines, teases and leads.

BEHAVIOR MODIFICATION: For the purposes of this book, behavior modification is the act of doing something that isn't a strength or comfortable for you, long enough so that it eventually becomes second nature.

CLOSED THROW (TOSS): A closed throw ends with a closed statement or the reporter's name. A closed throw is complete and doesn't require an answer or a response.

COMMAND ANCHOR, THE: Along with mastering the Anchor Paradigm, the Command Anchor must be a Gracious Host, the Omniscient Observer, the Viewer's Representative, the Devil's Advocate, the Expert and the Viewer's Protector.

CONDITIONAL COPY: Writing that includes words such as 'some,' 'may,' 'might,' 'should,' 'could,' 'usually,' 'possibly,' and 'probably' when it causes the message to be indecisive or ambiguous.

DILETTANTE: A person who cultivates an area of interest without real commitment or knowledge.   An amateur who pretends to be very knowledgeable.

DOUBLE HOOK, THE: A tease with two beats, each of which hooks the viewer.

EMOTIONAL TONE: The emotional quality of the voice – loving, harsh, compassionate, sarcastic – that sets the mood of a word, phrase or story.

EVENTS LIST: A comprehensive list of events to use during weather tosses associated with holidays, kids, the home and the car that will make those interactions human condition oriented, substantive and viewer-centric.

"GOD IS IN THE DETAIL":   The quote, meaning that whatever task is taken on should be done thoroughly, has been attributed to various individuals, but mostly to the German-born architect Ludwig Mies van der Rohe.

GRATUITOUS THANK YOU: The use of "Thank you" as nothing more than a bridge to get from one thing to the next, uttering it in such an off-handed and absent-minded way that it comes across as by rote, dismissive and insincere.

HARD NEWS: Content usually found at the top of a newscast that deals with serious subjects such as war, crime, death, politics, and economics.

HELPING VERBS: Also known as Auxiliary Verbs are forms of the verbs, "be," "do," "have," and "will," when followed by another verb in order to form a question, a negative sentence, a compound tense, or the passive. Helping verbs have a tendency to weaken the message and should be avoided when writing headlines, teases and leads.

HERO'S JOURNEY: The mythology story structure, broken down into eleven stages, most cultures throughout history follow as theorized by Joseph Campbell in his book, *The Hero with a Thousand Faces*. The seven stages are: 1) The Call to Adventure, 2) Refusal of the Call, 3) Meeting the Mentor, 4) Crossing the Threshold, 5) Tests, 6) Approaching the innermost Cave, 7) Ordeal, 8) Reward/Bliss, 9) The Road Back, 10) Resurrection, 11) Master of Two Worlds.

HIGH CONCEPT: A word, phrase or sentence that tells you everything you need to know about what you are going to experience.

HUMAN CONDITION, THE: The totality of human behavioral patterns, ideas and attitudes. Life's events and encounters that are susceptible to or representative of a human beings' sympathies, passions, and feelings. The conscious understanding of good and evil, spirit and mortality.

HYPERBOLIC ADJECTIVE: A word that describes or modifies another word in an exaggerated or overstated way. Words like 'bizarre,' 'fantastic,' 'astonishing,' and 'unbelievable,' should only be used in copy if they are literal and not subjective.

IDEAL INTERACTION: Interaction that moves the show forward. It educates, elevates, and motivates. It is concise, confident, viewer-centric as opposed to egocentric, adds information or perspective, each statement moves the show forward, reveals your personality, shows co-anchors in a good light, avoids one or two-word affirmations, and builds strong relationships with teammates as well as the viewer

INSTITUTIONAL WRITING: Copy that begins with data instead of the human condition. Headlines, teases and leads that begin with names, numbers, titles and organizations are generally considered institutional.

LEAD (Lede), THE: The beginning sentence or paragraph of a news story is called 'the lead.'

LIVE SHOT: A 'remote' or a 'live remote' or a 'live shot' is broadcasting done from a location away from the news station or television studio.

LOOK LIVE: A 'Live Shot' that was actually taped ahead of time (prior to airtime), but is aired during the show as if it were happening in real time.

MEMORABLE MOMENT: A moment during the newscast that creates a lasting impression for the viewer.

NEUTRAL ZONE: The area between your waist and your chest. When your hands are in the Neutral Zone and moving naturally, they are the least distracting and can be the most effective.

OCM: The Weather Channel's acronym for an on-camera meteorologist.

OPEN THROW (TOSS): An open-ended throw is one that initiates interaction or gives the impression that the reporter is being motivated by what the anchor has just said to continue in the same vain. An open throw can be a question or an open statement.

PASSIVE VOICE: The receiver of the action usually precedes the verb, i.e., *"The boy was bitten by the hungry lion."* The simple formula for writing in the passive voice is, OBJECT – VERB – NOUN.

PERSONALITY: A person's set of characteristics: the totality of a person's attitudes, interests, behavioral patterns, emotional responses, social roles, and other individual traits that endure over long periods of time.

PERSPECTIVE: Information relative to the viewer's reality and sensibilities that makes the subject that much clearer by its presence. Perspective makes the story or question or subject more important by siding it up to relative news matters.

RESEARCH VERBATIMS: Research projects will sometimes poll a group of individuals that mirror the market's target viewers in an effort to ascertain their thoughts and feelings about a news station's product. Research verbatims are word-for-word transcripts of each individual's comments in the group or their answers to specific research questions.

RESONANCE: The type of sound your voice produces when it reverberates from different areas of your head and chest.

ROMANTIC REALITY: TV and film's portrayal of life as a heightened sense of reality with all of the foibles removed. It shows the viewer what life could or should be instead of how it actually is.

SEVEN BASIC PLOTS, THE: Christopher Booker's book which suggests that any story you hear follows one of (or a combination of) seven scenarios: 1) Rags to Riches, 2) The Quest, 3) Voyage and Return, 4) Comedy, 5) Tragedy, 6) Rebirth, 7) Overcoming the Monster.

SING-SONG: A monotonous cadence or a repeated rising and falling pitch or rhythm of the speaking voice.

SOFT COPY: Writing that is indecisive, nebulous, boring, unexciting, stagnant, and institutional.

SOT: An acronym for 'sound on tape.' In film it refers to any ambient sound captured during the time of recording as opposed to adding sound later in post-production. In broadcast news it usually refers to audio captured from an individual or individuals on camera, also known as a soundbite.

STAND UP, THE: Appearing in front of the camera to introduce, narrate or tag a story.

SUBCONSCIOUS, THE: This can be a very powerful tool if used properly. It does what you tell it. It doesn't like avoidance. And it will mold you into the character you tell others you have.

SUBJECTIVE ADJECTIVE: A word that describes or modifies another word based on your own idea or opinion rather than fact.

TARGET (VIEWER) DEMOGRAPHIC: The specific audience member or consumer group stations gear their shows towards, based mainly on age, gender and income.

VERBATIMS, RESEARCH: Research projects will sometimes poll a group of individuals that mirror the market's target viewers in an effort to ascertain their thoughts and feelings about a news station's product. Research verbatims are word-for-word transcripts of each individual's comments in the group or their answers to specific research questions.

VOICE COLOR: Making words sound like what they mean in that context. For example, saying "fast" quickly, "slow" drawn out, "explosion" with a pop, and "sleepy" in a soft and soothing voice are all instances of using voice color.

ACKNOWLEDGMENTS

For the last 37 years, Stacy Widelitz has been a trusted compatriot, strong ally, and best friend. His council keeps me balanced and his sense of humor keeps me sane.

News Director extraordinaire Sandy Boonstra has been a great friend and confidant for 24 years. Her ability to maintain honesty and integrity in a business that makes it damn near impossible, has been an inspiration.

Melissa Core and Rick Caballo are wickedly talented and brilliant at everything they put their minds to. I trust them with my business, cherish them as my friends, and love them like family.

About four years after the World Wide Web became publicly available, I had the incredibly good fortune to meet and become friends with Gary Fieldsend; a man with a great heart, uplifting spirit, and who is crazy genius with all things computer related. Through the years he has been invaluable as my internet mentor, web-site creator, and trusted foil for each one of my books. I am truly a lucky man to have Gary as a confidant and as a friend.

I am grateful to Michael Gomez, such an amazing photographer, for his art, his support and his friendship.

There are folks that have been instrumental in my success in the Broadcast News game business. Barry Davis has been a client, great friend and a huge supporter for much of my career.

He has won an embarrassing number of Emmys and accolades as a reporter and anchor, yet I think we both know who actually deserves to have his name on all of those awards. (Just kidding, Barry. You deserve it ALL and more, my friend.)

In the Broadcast News game, the station's news director is usually the person who hires the talent coach. However, there are two Vice President General Managers that I want to thank for championing me since the 1990's until present day. Greg McAlister and Ken Selvaggi; two gentlemen that have always had such a strength of character and clear vision to be formattable leaders. It has been a privilege to work for them and an honor to call them my friends.

With all my respect and admiration, these folks have also given me an incredible amount of support and guidance throughout my career. To Bill Hooper for his positive energy and kindness, to C.J. Beutien for his staunch commitment to the work and support of all those anchors, reporters and producers working for him. To my good friend Dan Fabrizio for our long discussions and collaborations in a constant pursuit of excellence. To Kelly Groft, whose intelligence and humanity always motivates me to be on my best game. To Russ Poteet whose understanding of the human condition and generosity of spirit nurtures everyone around him. I also want to thank Skip Valet and Tom Doerr for showing me a kindness and belief so early in my career.

Most successful folks can point to a seminal moment in their lives when they suddenly found themselves on the path towards mastery. Mine came in the way of the fabulous Florence M. Sikes. She saw a talent in me when I was twelve years of age and continued to champion that talent, mentoring me to be the best, first as an actor, then as a director, and finally as a talent coach, for the next 39 years, until her passing. She gave me mountains of knowledge, to be sure. But her real gift to me was the confidence that I was good enough and smart enough and that I deserved to be the best. I am grateful to this day, honored and blessed to have had the opportunity to know, love and cherish such a rare soul.

INDEX

V

valuable beyond the content · 13, 100, 106
VALUABLE   BEYOND   THE CONTENT · 13
value beyond the content · 15, 95, 142
VALUE BEYOND THE CONTENT · 5, 12, 134
VERBATIMS · 156, 157
VHS · 8
video · 8, 29, 81, 121, 127, 132
viewer · 11, 23, 26, 32, 33, 34, 35, 36, 37, 41, 43, 44, 50, 54, 55, 58, 59, 65, 66, 67, 70, 71, 74, 78, 79, 81, 83, 84, 87, 95, 97, 98, 99, 100, 102, 103, 106, 108, 109, 110, 111, 112, 113, 114, 115, 117, 118, 122, 123, 124, 125, 126, 128, 129, 131, 132, 134, 138, 139, 140, 141, 143, 145, 146, 147, 149, 151, 152, 154, 155, 156
viewer(s) · 108, 110
Viewer's Representative, The · 111
Viewer-centric · 96
viewers · 6, 8, 9, 11, 12, 13, 23, 30, 31, 41, 51, 54, 55, 61, 62, 66, 67, 70, 71, 72, 73, 74, 82, 83, 86, 87, 94, 95, 96, 98, 99, 106, 107, 108, 111, 112, 113, 114, 122, 123, 127, 128, 132, 134, 135, 136, 139, 140, 142, 143, 146, 147, 156, 157
vision · 22, 160
visual · 29, 30, 32, 37, 50, 54, 55, 83, 141
visual image · 29, 30, 83
Visualize · 29
vocal quality · 22, 83, 85, 86
vocal resonance · 84
vocal variety · 13, 22, 32, 33, 42, 71, 74, 75, 80, 84, 85, 130

Vocal warm-up · 86
voice · 3, 30, 31, 58, 71, 73, 74, 75, 76, 78, 80, 83, 84, 85, 98, 108, 125, 130, 151, 152, 155, 156, 157
Voice color · 76
VOICE COLOR · 157

W

walk-and-talk · 129
WARDROBE · 35
weather · 12, 13, 113, 114, 115, 133, 134, 135, 136, 138, 139, 140, 141, 142, 143, 145, 146, 147, 152
Weather Channel · 134, 135, 136, 137, 155
weather condition · 12
weathercaster · 1, 12, 20, 31, 39, 66, 95, 100, 114, 115, 142, 143, 149
Weathercaster · 134, 139
WEATHERCASTER · 114, 133, 145
weathercasters · 3, 94, 95, 114, 134, 141, 142, 143, 146
Weathercasters · 15, 135, 139
West Side Story · 39
Westerners · 86
Work takes the time allotted · 9
world-wide web · 8
write · 9, 45, 50, 52, 55, 56, 80, 149
writer · 49, 51, 73, 74, 79, 91, 121
writers · 44, 49, 79

Y

Yogi the Bear · 93

Z

Zen · 19, 20